THE LITTLE BLUE THINKING BOOK

50

POWERFUL
PRINCIPLES FOR
CLEAR AND EFFECTIVE
THINKING

BRANDON ROYAL

FALL RIVER PRESS

New York

FALL RIVER PRESS

New York

An Imprint of Sterling Publishing
387 Park Avenue South
New York, NY 10016

FALL RIVER PRESS and the distinctive Fall River Press logo
are registered trademarks of Barnes & Noble, Inc.

This 2013 edition published by Fall River Press by arrangement with Maven Publishing.

ISBN 978-1-4351-4568-9

Distributed in Canada by Sterling Publishing
c/o Canadian Manda Group, 165 Dufferin Street
Toronto, Ontario, Canada M6K 3H6
Distributed in the United Kingdom by GMC Distribution Services
Castle Place, 166 High Street, Lewes, East Sussex, England BN7 1XU
Distributed in Australia by Capricorn Link (Australia) Pty. Ltd.
P.O. Box 704, Windsor, NSW 2756, Australia

For information about custom editions, special sales, and premium and corporate purchases,
please contact Sterling Special Sales at 800-805-5489 or specialsales@sterlingpublishing.com.

Manufactured in China

2 4 6 8 10 9 7 5 3

www.sterlingpublishing.com

Contents

Preface   5

Introduction   6

Quiz   8

CHAPTER 1: Perception and Mindset

Selective Perception   13

The Magic of Coincidence   14

The Four Classic Mindsets   16

CHAPTER 2: Creative Thinking

Overview   25

Lateral Thinking   25

Divergent vs. Convergent Thinking   31

Mind Maps   35

Devil's Advocate Technique   39

Idea Killers and Idea Growers   40

Brainstorming   46

Reframing Problems   50

Selling Creative Ideas   52

CHAPTER 3: Decision Making

Overview   55

Pros-and-Cons Analysis   56

Matrixes   62

Decision-Event Trees   72

Probability Trees   77

Weighted Ranking   77

Utility Analysis   84

Sunk Costs   86

Hypothesis Testing   88
Prisoner's Dilemma   95

CHAPTER 4: Analyzing Arguments
Overview   101
The ABCs of Argument Structure   102
Evaluating Arguments   103
The Five Common Reasoning Flaws   109
Testing Critical Reasoning   120
Putting It All Together   134

CHAPTER 5: Mastering Logic
Overview   137
"If...Then" Statements   138
"No-Some-Most-All" Statements   141
Mutual Inclusivity and Exclusivity   142
Statements of Logical Equivalency   144
Testing Logic-based Reasoning   146

Appendix I—Summary of Reasoning Tips 1 to 50   155
Appendix II—Fallacious Reasoning   159
Appendix III—Avoiding Improper Inferences   169
Appendix IV—Analogies   171
Appendix V—The Ten Classic Trade-offs   175
Appendix VI—Critical Reading and Comprehension   182
Appendix VII—Tips for Taking Reading Tests   185
Answers and Explanations   201
Quiz—Answers   253
Selected Bibliography   256
Index   258
About the Author   262

Preface

Henry Humidor purchased a box of very rare, very expensive cigars and insured them, among other things, against fire. Within a month, having smoked his entire stockpile of cigars, he filed a claim against the insurance company. In his claim, Henry stated the cigars were lost "in a series of small fires." The insurance company refused to pay, citing the obvious reason: He had consumed the cigars in the normal fashion.

Henry sued and won!

In delivering the ruling, the judge agreed that the claim was frivolous. He stated that the man nevertheless held a policy from the company in which it had warranted that the cigars were insurable and also guaranteed that it would insure against fire, without adequately defining what is considered to be an "unacceptable fire," and was obligated to pay the claim.

Rather than endure a lengthy and costly appeals process, the insurance company accepted the ruling and paid Henry $15,000 for the rare cigars he lost in the "fires."

But...

After Henry cashed the check, the insurance company had him arrested on twenty-four counts of arson! With his own insurance claim and testimony from the previous case used against him, Henry Humidor was convicted of intentionally setting fire to his insured property and was sentenced to twenty-four months in jail and a $24,000 fine.

Welcome to the wonderful world of reasoning.

Introduction

Some 2,500 years ago, Socrates gave birth to the art and science of what we now call critical reasoning. Through a system of inquiry, known as the "Socratic method," Socrates used a series of probing questions to obtain answers and then critique those answers. In this manner, he sought to reveal the key issues behind perplexing problems, to uncover the merit and flaws in commonly held ideas, and to expose those contradictory beliefs that often hide behind smooth-sounding, but empty, rhetoric. It is indeed humorous to reflect on Socrates' observation that one cannot necessarily rely on the "sound" judgment of those individuals occupying positions of authority; they may be prone to think in a muddled, whimsical, or irrational manner.

Critical reasoning, also referred to as critical thinking, may be defined broadly as "the process by which we evaluate information." Often, the information we seek relates to problems or opportunities, and the process relates to how we arrive at our conclusions based upon the information we have. Individuals who possess critical thinking skills can identify problems or opportunities, gather relevant information, analyze information in a "proper" way, and come to reliable conclusions by themselves, without necessarily relying on others.

Notwithstanding our ability to read, no other single skill is more important than our ability to reason. Yet, strangely, no required course dedicated to reasoning skills exists as a part of our regular school curriculum or as part of any on-the-job training program. This book provides a distillation of the most useful academic and real-life reasoning concepts. Teaching in our school systems—primary, secondary, and post-secondary—has traditionally been skewed toward instructing us "what to think" as opposed to "how to think." An all-rounded education must balance the teaching of course content with new and better ways of understanding and interpreting the material at hand.

This book contains fifty reasoning tips interspersed throughout five sections. **Perception and Mindset (*Chapter 1*)** provides an initial framework for reasoning. We live in a world of imperfect information and of imperfect abilities, where subjectivity is a key ingredient. As no two individuals have the same perspective or mindset, we must make allowances for this when mastering the tools of reasoning and logic.

Creative Thinking (*Chapter 2*) introduces non-traditional thinking methods. Creative thinking is non-linear thinking and is often referred to as "out-of-the-box" thinking. One of the most useful topics is reframing problems. An important step in problem solving involves asking, "Is the perceived problem really the problem?" The ability to use creativity to better define problems bolsters our ability to solve problems.

Decision Making (*Chapter 3*) focuses on applied reasoning and introduces various tools, the major benefit of which is to structure or quantify the decision-making process. The basic tools—"boxes" and "trees"—are devices that allow problems to be approached in an efficient, organized manner. Other tools, such as weighted ranking and utility analysis, allow us to quantify qualitative decisions (e.g., hiring decisions, career choices), which may or may not involve monetary considerations.

Analyzing Arguments (*Chapter 4*) shows us how to break arguments down according to classic argument structure: conclusion, evidence, and assumption. The ability to understand, attack, and defend arguments is one of the most fundamental uses of reasoning skills. **Mastering Logic (*Chapter 5*)** contains some of the more technical material in this book, but it also provides the foundation for understanding some of the most relevant examples of reasoning flaws found in everyday conversation and speech.

Let's get started.

Quiz

Try these ten basic, but occasionally tricky, reasoning concepts. Mark each statement as being either true or false. Answers can be found on pages 253–255 of this book.

1. Left-brain thinking might be described as "floodlight" thinking, while right-brain thinking might be described as "spotlight" thinking.

   ❏ True   ❏ False

2. The following represents the formulaic relationship among the three elements of classic argument structure: Evidence − Assumption = Conclusion.

   ❏ True   ❏ False

3. The statement "some doctors are rich people" does not imply reciprocality because "some rich people might not be doctors."

   ❏ True   ❏ False

4. The ad hominem fallacy consists in attempting to hide a weakness by drawing attention away from the real issue and emphasizing a side issue.

   ❏ True   ❏ False

5. In formal logic, the statement "Every A is a B" may be translated as "Only As are Bs."

   ❏ True   ❏ False

6. The halo effect occurs when a person so wishes something to be true that, in his or her mind, the situation is believed to be true.

   ❏ True   ❏ False

7. The words "inference" and "assumption" may be used interchangeably.

   ❏ True   ❏ False

8. The beauty of matrixes lies in their ability to summarize data across rows and columns. However, data must be "collectively exclusive and mutually exhaustive."

   ❏ True   ❏ False

9. Utility analysis takes into account the desirability of outcomes by multiplying a given value by the probability of its occurrence; all resultant values will total to 100%.

   ❏ True   ❏ False

10. The Prisoner's Dilemma provides an example of how competition is superior to cooperation.

   ❏ True   ❏ False

Chapter 1

Perception and Mindset

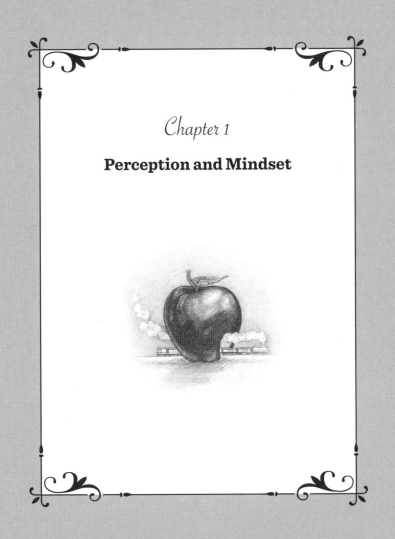

*Many complain about their memory,
few about their judgment.*

—LA ROCHEFOUCAULD

Selective Perception

Tip #1: Selective perception is the tendency to see the world the way we would like it to be rather than how it really is. The sound thinker suspends judgment and is not unduly influenced by stereotypes, prejudices, isolated experiences, or preconceived notions.

Imagine recovering your sight after thirty years of blindness. Pioneering psychologist K. F. Muenzinger captured the words of a person who had made this remarkable journey:

> When I could see again, objects seemed to hurl themselves at me. One of the things normal people know from long habit is what not to look at. Things that don't matter, or that confuse, are simply shut out of their minds. I had forgotten this, and tried to see everything at once; consequently I saw almost nothing.

This interesting but extreme case is virtually the opposite of what most of us typically experience in our thinking. The active thinker struggles to gain more latitude, differing viewpoints, and corroborating information. We hardly worry about seeing too much, but rather about seeing too little. All-rounded thinking—thinking that encompasses both sides of an issue or topic—is probably the greatest asset that training in critical thinking can lend us.

Age, culture, gender, education, and work and life experience are major reasons why no two individuals see the world in exactly the same way. Perhaps the most basic way to view the world is from a positive or negative perspective. Is the cup half full or half empty? Are we perennial pessimists or incurable optimists?

Consider the following truncated profiles that describe the life and times of Remus Reid. Folklore has it that two separate newspaper accounts surfaced regarding the death of cowboy Remus Reid—one from the sheriff's office and one from a close relative who lived in Remus' hometown:

From the sheriff's office:

> *"Remus Reid, horse thief, sent to prison in 1885, escaped in 1887, robbed the local train six times. Caught by local detectives, convicted and hanged in 1889."*

From Remus' doting relative:

> *"Remus Reid was a famous cowboy whose business empire grew to include acquisition of valuable equestrian assets and intimate dealings with the regional railroad. Beginning in 1883, he devoted several years of his life to government service, finally taking leave to resume his dealings with the railroad. In 1887, he was a key player in a vital legal investigation. In 1889, Remus passed away during an important civic function held in his honor when the platform upon which he was standing collapsed."*

We have a tendency to interpret events selectively. If we want things to be "this way" or "that way" we can most certainly select, stack, or arrange evidence in a way that supports such a viewpoint.

Selective perception is based on what seems to us to stand out. However, what seems to us to be standing out may very well be related to our goals, interests, expectations, past experiences, or current demands of the situation—"with a hammer in hand, everything looks like a nail." The preceding quote highlights the phenomenon of selective perception. If we want to use a hammer, then the world around us may begin to look as though it is full of nails!

The Magic of Coincidence

Ponder this rather astounding comparison of the assassinations of two famous American presidents:

- ❖ Abraham Lincoln was elected to Congress in 1846.
  John F. Kennedy was elected to Congress in 1946.

- ❖ Abraham Lincoln was elected president in 1860.
  John F. Kennedy was elected president in 1960.

❖ The names Lincoln and Kennedy each contain seven letters.

❖ Both were particularly concerned with civil rights.

❖ Both wives lost children while living in the White House.

❖ Both presidents were shot on a Friday. Both were shot in the head.

❖ Lincoln's secretary was named Kennedy. Kennedy's secretary was named Lincoln.

❖ Both were assassinated by Southerners. Both were succeeded by Southerners. Both successors were named Johnson.

❖ Andrew Johnson, who succeeded Lincoln, was born in 1808. Lyndon Johnson, who succeeded Kennedy, was born in 1908.

❖ John Wilkes Booth, who assassinated Lincoln, was born in 1839. Lee Harvey Oswald, who assassinated Kennedy, was born in 1939.

❖ Both assassins were known by their three names. The names of both assassins comprise fifteen letters.

❖ Booth ran from a theatre and was caught in a warehouse. Oswald ran from a warehouse and was caught in a theatre.

❖ Booth and Oswald were both assassinated before their trials.

❖ A week before Lincoln was shot he was in Monroe, Maryland. A year before Kennedy was shot he was with Marilyn Monroe.

Despite how enticing the above comparison may appear, we must keep in mind that there are likely just as many differences as there are similarities between these two events. Care must be exercised so as to not overestimate the veracity of such a compilation. Recall the well-known saying: "If a billion chimpanzees were to sit down in front of a billion computers with a billion hours to spare, eventually one of them would type Tolstoy's *War and Peace*." Eventually one chimpanzee would arrange the letters exactly as they appear in that novel—typing the identical letters to form those identical words, in the right order, with the right spaces, and the correct punctuation. Here, the magic of chance or coincidence reminds us that almost anything is possible.

Here's some offhanded Commonwealth humor:

Year 1981:

- ❖ Prince Charles got married.
- ❖ Liverpool crowned Champions of Europe.
- ❖ Australia lost the Ashes tournament.
- ❖ The Pope died.

Year 2005:

- ❖ Prince Charles got married.
- ❖ Liverpool crowned Champions of Europe.
- ❖ Australia lost the Ashes tournament.
- ❖ The Pope died.

Lesson learned: The next time Prince Charles gets married, would someone please warn the Pope?

At the crossroads of selective perception and coincidence is something known as the "halo effect." The halo effect is the tendency to view a person, place, or thing favorably based on only a single incident, trait, or characteristic. For example, if someone arrives at our firm to answer a job ad and happens to be impeccably dressed, we may view this person favorably and overlook certain technical qualifications required for the job. Sometimes the halo effect is tied to coincidence. Say, for example, the candidate who arrives at our company for an interview happens to be from our hometown. Perhaps they also know someone we know. These coincidences may cause us to view the candidate favorably in an overall way.

The Four Classic Mindsets

Each of us learns early that different people see the world differently. Our experience, background, and predispositions play a unique role in shaping our outlook. Ponder this simple but revealing question:

Which of the following five sports is least like the other four?

A) Baseball
B) Cricket
C) Soccer (Football)
D) Golf
E) Ice Hockey

This is indeed an interesting question highlighting the possibility of multiple solutions and subjective interpretations. Not only would such a question never be chosen for an IQ test, but it also hints at ambiguity so often present whenever individuals make choices.

Most people find themselves choosing choice D insofar as golf is primarily an individual sport while the other sports are team sports. Golf is also the only sport here in which a lower score beats a higher score. Some pontificate whether the distinction rests on the degree to which golf is more mental than physical while the other four sports are more physical than mental. Certainly physical speed is of obvious importance in all sports except golf. Choice E is likely the next most popular. Ice hockey is essentially a winter sport, whereas the other sports are typically played in warmer weather. In ice hockey, players use skates, whereas in the other sports players use sporting shoes. Ice hockey is also played with a puck, the others, with balls! (Pun intended—ice hockey is notorious for being one of the roughest of sports and the only one listed above where you can legitimately "check" another player.)

A number of people see soccer (football) as least like the other three. After all, the other sports are played with stick-like objects: golf requires clubs, irons, and putters; ice hockey requires sticks, and baseball and cricket require bats. Football (soccer) also is played with an air-filled object, not a solid ball or puck.

People who choose choice A point to the fact that baseball has no true world championship—the "World Series" is an American phenomenon. Choice B (cricket) represents a sport that is played primarily in Commonwealth countries.

Every answer choice is both right and wrong! In summary, there are at least four distinct ways in which individuals draw broad contrasts among these different sports. Some people tend to focus first on the *number of people* who play the sport (individual vs. team sport), some focus on the *speed* with which each sport is played (walking vs. running), some focus on the *objects used* to play the sport (puck vs. ball, inflatable object vs. non-inflatable object, stick-like object vs. non-stick-like object), while others see these sports in the context of *when* (winter vs. summer, cold weather vs. warm weather) or *where* they are played (within a particular country or region).

In terms of thinking about how different people think, it is useful to massage the concept of "mindset." Many schemas exist which seek to classify mindsets. For instance, if we were to spend time reviewing how various people choose an answer to the above multiple-choice question, we might find the following: some people are more analytical, some more holistic, some are more results-oriented, and some are more process-oriented. Case in point: People who are analytically minded tend to focus on the instruments used to play the sport. People who are holistically minded tend to see the sport in terms of when and where (i.e., geography) it is played. People who are results-oriented are more likely to see the end result, contrasting the desirable low scores in golf with the desirable high scores in the other four sports. Process-oriented individuals will likely see contrasts in the number of players who play each sport, their physical size, and their athletic movements.

Tip #2: Think of mindsets as divided into four basic types: Analysts, Idealists, Realists, and Synthesists. These mindsets can be further contrasted based on levels of practicality and emotional attachment.

Our natural dispositions with respect to how we see the world come with their inherent strengths and weaknesses. Such dispositions, often referred to as mindsets, can help us in understanding how others around us are motivated.

To understand the importance of mindsets, ponder why it might be difficult, apart from obvious time constraints, to be a movie actor, director, and producer—all at the same time. The answer lies in competing skills and personalities. An actor needs to be dynamic and spontaneous, a director needs to be systematic and creative, and a producer needs to be persuasive, commercial, and administrative.

The list below summarizes the four mindsets of the Realist, Idealist, Analyst, and Synthesist.

Realist: Describes a person whose primary goal is "getting the job done" (results oriented).

Idealist: Describes a person whose primary goal is "finding the 'right' answer" (process oriented).

Analyst: Describes a person whose primary goal is "obtaining a thorough evaluation" (analytically oriented).

Synthesist: Describes a person whose primary goal is "achieving a composite view" (holistically oriented).

Exhibit 1.1 on the following page may be used to further contrast the four classic mindsets in terms of *practicality* and *emotion*. In short, Realists and Analysts are deemed more practical than Idealists or Synthesists (this is fairly empirical). Also, Realists and Idealists are deemed to be more emotional than are Analysts or Synthesists. Realists and Idealists tend to deal more with people in moving their goals forward. Realists know where they are going and need to enlist people's help, while Idealists seek to marshal support in determining the proper course of action. On the other hand, Analysts and Synthesists favor the intellectual more than the emotional. The Analyst deals with details—the pieces of the puzzle at hand—while the Synthesist tries to draw themes from the information presented; thus, there is less need for emotional attachment.

Exhibit 1.1 The Four Classic Mindsets

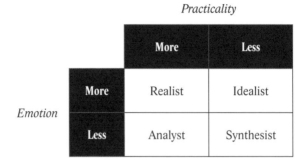

Practicality

		More	Less
Emotion	**More**	Realist	Idealist
	Less	Analyst	Synthesist

Exhibit 1.2 presents a stereotypical list of traits for individuals working across different fields. Naturally, a "good" thinker must not be unduly influenced by such stereotypes.

Exhibit 1.2 Perceptions of the Professions

	Perceived Strengths	Perceived Weaknesses
1. Accountant	• Good technical, quantitative skills • Good at reality checks • Diligent	• Not dynamic; not a leader • Lacks big-picture view despite exposure to different industries
2. Administrator/Personnel	• Organized; detail minded • Trained to take care of people; team player	• Doesn't know how to build a business • Stuck on rules and procedures

Exhibit 1.2 *(Cont'd)*

	Perceived Strengths	Perceived Weaknesses
3. Artist	• Flexible mindset; creative • Unique viewpoint	• Not quantitatively skilled • Doesn't know how to manage people
4. Computer/ Internet/ Techno Geek	• Quantitatively skilled • Understands technology and uses hands-on approach	• Lacks people skills • Lacks big-picture view
5. Consultant	• Can think outside the box; good business sense • Articulate; smart	• Doesn't care about detail • Too theoretical; too much style at the expense of substance
6. Engineer	• Methodical; hardworking • Quantitatively and technologically skilled	• Myopic; can't see the forest for the trees • Lacks communication skills
7. Entrepreneur	• Dynamic; high energy level • Hands on; a real doer	• Chaotic; disorganized; easily bored; impatient • Averse to theory

Exhibit 1.2 *(Cont'd)*

	Perceived Strengths	Perceived Weaknesses
8. Investment Banker	• Savvy; resourceful; knows the bottom line; good at networking • Facility with numbers	• Callous; uncaring; arrogant • Focuses on the "ends" at the expense of the "means"
9. Lawyer	• Smart; clever communicator • Well trained; good organizational skills	• Works alone; set in his or her ways • Not quantitatively skilled
10. Marketer/ Salesperson	• Strong personality; self-confident • Understands the consumer	• Lacks number sense • Doesn't see value in theory or book learning
11. Military	• Obeys rules; disciplined • Team player	• Commercial misfit • Too focused on executing orders; not enough vision
12. Scientist	• Intelligent; unique viewpoint • Quantitatively skilled	• Lacks business sense; inhibited • Can't "bullshit"; unwilling to develop soft skills

Chapter 2

Creative Thinking

Our task, regarding creativity, is to help children climb their own mountains, as high as possible. No one can do more than that.

—LORIS MALAGUZZI

Overview

Loosely speaking, there are two types of thinking—analytical and creative. Analytical thinking is the focus of *Chapters 3*, *4*, and *5*. Because so much emphasis is typically placed on traditional, analytical problem-solving techniques, this chapter "reverses the order" and precedes with non-traditional, creative techniques for use in analyzing and solving problems.

Lateral thinking, an offshoot of creative thinking, is discussed first. The problems titled *Stroke*, *Pattern*, and *Nine Dots* are examples of puzzles that highlight the power of programmed responses. As a follow-up, we explore differences between convergent thinking and divergent thinking and the strengths and weaknesses of both abilities. The primary goal is to broaden the mind and develop an all-around thinking process.

Because fresh ideas are the bloodline of creativity, a discussion of how to generate ideas includes sections on brainstorming as well as "idea growers" and "idea killers." In terms of solving problems, the technique of reframing problems to determine whether the problem is really the problem is an extremely valuable tool.

Finally, we address some issues regarding the "selling" of creative ideas within the context of organizations, where other individuals will have an impact on the success or failure of those ideas being presented.

Lateral Thinking

Tip #3: Creative thinking is "backdoor" thinking.

Creative thinking is often used synonymously with the term "lateral" thinking. Although lateral thinking is not a new term, Dr. Edward De Bono was the person who coined it, and much of the term's popularity has arisen from his book of the same title. Here are some differences between traditional or "vertical" thinking and creative or lateral thinking.

Traditional or Vertical Thinking	Creative or Lateral Thinking
• Traditional thinking is straightforward thinking.	• Creative thinking is sideways thinking.
• Traditional thinking is front-door thinking.	• Creative thinking is back-door thinking.
• Traditional thinking is logical thinking.	• Creative thinking is spontaneous thinking.
• Traditional thinking is high-probability thinking.	• Creative thinking is low-probability thinking.
• Traditional thinking is primarily left-brain thinking.	• Creative thinking is primarily right-brain thinking.
• Traditional thinking is "inside-the-box" thinking.	• Creative thinking is "outside-the-box" thinking.
• Traditional thinking is like a river that follows a set course.	• Creative thinking is like a river that overflows and moves in new directions.

The concept of creative thinking is somewhat more difficult to describe than to illustrate. The following story suffices as a noteworthy example.

> Many years ago, a hapless merchant owed a substantial sum
> of money to a wealthy moneylender. Unable to pay back his
> debt, the merchant knew that the moneylender could see to it
> that he was put in jail.
>
> The moneylender was old, ugly, and ill-tempered, but
> he couldn't help but notice how beautiful the merchant's

teenage daughter was. He proposed a deal to relinquish the debt and ensure that the daughter would not starve as a result of her father's going to jail.

The moneylender said he would place two small stones, one white and one black, into an empty money-bag and permit the splendid young lady to choose her fate. If she reached into the bag and chose the white stone, her father's debt would be canceled and she would be free from any obligation to marry him. If the stone was black, the father's debt would be canceled, but the young girl would have to marry the moneylender. If she refused to choose, the father would immediately go to jail.

Horrified by their present predicament, the father and daughter knew they could not refuse the moneylender's proposal for debt relief.

Soon the moment of truth had arrived. The three of them met on the garden path of the moneylender's large home. The moneylender bent over to pick up two small rocks. The girl grimaced with fright upon noticing that the moneylender had picked up two small rocks, both of them black, which he now placed in the money bag.

What would you have done if you had been the unfortunate girl? If you had been asked to advise her, what would you have told her to do? You may believe that careful, logical analysis would solve the problem, if there were a solution. This type of traditional, straightforward thinking is not much help to the girl in this story. In this respect, there are but two possibilities:

1. The girl should take a black pebble and sacrifice herself in order to save her father from prison.
2. The girl should refuse to choose a pebble, show that there are two black pebbles in the bag, expose the moneylender as a cheat, and demand a fair retrial.

This story shows the difference between traditional thinking and creative thinking. Traditional thinkers are concerned with the fact that the girl has to take the pebble and on how the parameters of the "game" are fixed. Creative thinkers are concerned with changing the focus or parameters of the game. Traditional thinkers take the reasonable view of a situation and then proceed logically and carefully to work it out. Creative thinkers tend to explore all the different ways of looking at something, rather than accepting the most promising and proceeding from that.

Here's how the story ends:

> "Please choose, my fair maiden," the moneylender said.
> The young woman reached into the money bag and pulled out a rock, which she purposefully let fall to the ground and disappear within the camouflage of the stone path beneath her. "How clumsy of me," she said, while looking toward the money-lender. "No matter though. If you look at the stone held in the bag, we'll be able to tell which color I must have chosen."
>
> With a sense of shock, and with no intention of admitting his dishonesty, the moneylender allowed the girl to reach back into the bag and reveal a black stone. "I chose the white stone!" the girl shouted with joy.

In this way, by using creative thinking, the girl changes what seems an impossible situation into an extremely advantageous one. The girl is actually better off than if the moneylender had been honest and had put one black and one white pebble into the bag, for then she would have had only an even chance of being saved. As it is, she is sure of remaining with her father and at the same time having his debt canceled. Creative thinking might result in two possibilities:

1. Before choosing, the girl should demand the opportunity to change colors, even offering to let the moneylender reach into the bag and choose a stone for her.

2. The girl should choose a stone, fumble it to the ground to conceal its color, and ask to see the color of the remaining stone in the money bag (just as she did in this story).

What types of things most hinder our ability to unleash creative thinking? The answer lies in distinguishing between programmed versus non-programmed responses.

Programmed responses are essential in everyday life, saving us from having to engage in deep thought in order to do routine tasks, e.g., going to the store, driving a car, or saying "hello" while anticipating a familiar response. However, programmed responses form barriers when we encounter novel situations, requiring non-programmed responses.

PROBLEM 1   ONE STROKE

Add one stroke or character to solve or make sense of the following:

$$IX = 6$$

Note: For answers and proposed solutions to exercises and problems, see the *Answers and Explanations* section that follows at the back of this book beginning on page 201.

PROBLEM 2   MOP

Make sense of the following: "The floor is dirty because Sally mopped it."

PROBLEM 3   PATTERN

Based on the pattern below, place each of the characters "E F G H I" in their proper position both above and below the line.

$$\frac{A}{B \quad C \quad D}$$

PROBLEM 4   NINE DOTS

Draw no more than four straight lines (without lifting the pencil or pen from the paper) in order to cross through all nine dots.

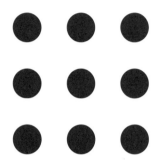

PROBLEM 5   TWO WATER BUCKETS

A circus owner sends one of his clowns to bring water back from a nearby river. The owner wants to mix the water with a special health concentrate to give to the elephants, and needs exactly seven gallons of water. He gives the clown a five-gallon bucket and a three-gallon bucket and tells him to bring back exactly seven gallons of water. How can the clown measure out exactly seven gallons of water using nothing but these two buckets and not guessing at the amount?

Five-Gallon   Three-Gallon
Bucket   Bucket

Divergent vs. Convergent Thinking

Tip #4: Convergent thinking focuses the mind; divergent thinking opens the mind.

At any point in the analytic process, from the very beginning to the very end, we are engaged in one of two thinking modes: convergent or divergent.

Convergence means bringing together and moving toward one point. Whenever we take a narrower view of a problem, focusing our mind on a single aspect of the puzzle, we are in a convergent mode. Whenever we take a broader view of a problem, whether by examining evidence more thoroughly, gathering new evidence, or entertaining alternative solutions, we are in a divergent mode.

While divergent thinking opens the mind to new ideas and thoughts, convergent thinking closes the mind by viewing a problem ever more narrowly until it focuses on—and produces—a single solution. An apt simile is a camera lens that can zoom in until the subject fills the aperture (convergence) or adjust to broaden the field of view around the subject (divergence). An even more dramatic contrast occurs when using a microscope or telescope.

Both divergence and convergence are necessary for effective problem solving. Divergence opens the mind to creative alternatives; convergence winnows out the weak alternatives, focusing on and choosing among the strong alternatives. Without divergence, we could not analyze a problem creatively or objectively; without convergence, we would just keep on analyzing, never coming to closure. It is therefore vital to effective problem solving that an individual be prepared to shift back and forth between divergent and convergent approaches easily and at will, using each mode to its best effect as the problem-solving process dictates.

Unfortunately, it is extremely difficult for individuals to shift back and forth between these two ever-opposite, ever-warring approaches.

Most of us are inherently better convergers than divergers. Divergence is not as instinctual as is convergence. Indeed, most of us habitually resist divergence—sometimes passionately, even angrily.

Discussion of divergent versus convergent thinking dovetails with the following overview of right-brain versus left-brain thinking.

In 1981, Dr. Roger Sperry was awarded the Nobel Prize for his proof of the split brain theory. Research confirmed that the brain has two hemispheres with different, but overlapping functions. The right and left hemispheres of the brain each specialize in distinct types of thinking processes. In the most basic sense, the left brain is the analytical side while the right brain is the creative side. In 95 percent of all right-handed people, the left side of the brain controls analytics while the right side controls creative endeavors. In most left-handed people, the hemisphere functions are reversed.

The passage below, relevant to the topic at hand, is excerpted from *The Little Red Writing Book*, where it is used to show how to structure written documents.

> *The left side of the brain is responsible for analytical, linear, verbal, and rational thought. Left-brain thinking is characterized as "spotlight" thinking. It is the left brain that a person relies on when balancing a checkbook, remembering names and dates, or setting goals and objectives.*
>
> *The right side of the brain is holistic, imaginative, non-verbal, and artistic. Right-brain thinking is characterized as "floodlight" thinking. Whenever a person recalls another person's face, becomes engrossed in a symphony, or simply daydreams, that person is engaged in right-brain functions.*
>
> *Since most of the Western concepts of thinking are derived from Greek logic, which is a linear logic system, left-brained processes are most rewarded in the Western education system. Right-brain processes are, to the chagrin of many, less often rewarded in school.*

The primary abilities of the left and right brain include:

Left Brain	Right Brain
• Analysis	• Artistic ability
• Classification	• Emotion
• Language	• Imagery
• Logic	• Imagination
• Memory	• Intuition
• Numbers	• Music
• Sequence	• Rhythm/Physical coordination
• Seriation	• Synthesis
• Writing	• Theatrics
• Convergent thinking processes	• Divergent thinking processes

Here is a snapshot summarizing left-brain and right-brain thinking:

Left-Brain Thinking	Right-Brain Thinking
• Left-brain thinking is characterized as "spotlight" thinking.	• Right-brain thinking is characterized as "floodlight" thinking.
• The functions of the left brain are characterized by sequence and order.	• The functions of the right brain are characterized as holistic and diffuse.
• The left brain can put the parts together into an organized whole.	• The right brain instinctively sees the whole, then the parts.
• The left hemisphere controls our analytical, scientific, logical, mathematical, and verbal leanings.	• The right hemisphere of the brain governs our artistic, musical, innovative, imaginative, entrepreneurial, political, theatrical, and visual tendencies.

Although it would be difficult, perhaps impossible, to find a task that requires the exclusive use of the right or left brain, the following exercise is an example of a strong right-brain activity. Reflect on the statement below and try to come up with at least six responses. You may write your answers on a separate sheet of paper.

How is a good idea like an iceberg?

Possible answers:

- ❖ A good idea is cool!
- ❖ A good idea stands out.
- ❖ A good idea may get a chilly reception.
- ❖ A good idea can easily disappear.
- ❖ Good ideas are fleeting.
- ❖ A good idea sure seems natural.
- ❖ A good idea has a big effect on its surroundings.
- ❖ A good idea takes time to form.
- ❖ Good ideas come in bunches.
- ❖ Good ideas are only created when conditions are right, and then, many are created.
- ❖ If you overlook a good idea, it can sink you.
- ❖ You have to go a long way to find a good idea.
- ❖ If you're looking in the wrong place, you'll never find one.
- ❖ You only see part of a good idea because there is more to it than meets the eye.
- ❖ There is a lot of depth in a good idea, but not everyone appreciates it.
- ❖ One-tenth of the benefit of a good idea is clearly visible, but nine-tenths of the long-term benefits lie below the surface.

Mind Maps

Mind maps, also generically known as concept maps or idea maps, are a note-taking technique that uses both visual and linear thought processes. They provide an alternative to traditional, linear note-taking skills. Tony Buzan is the best-known advocate and practitioner of concept maps, and although he didn't originate the technique, he did manage to come up with a name that sticks—mind maps!

The technique used to create mind maps is based on the workings of our bicameral brain (right and left side). The idea is that since linear note taking only appeals to one side of our brain, it would be more effective to take notes in such a manner as to appeal to both sides of our brain, thereby increasing retention and comprehension. Accordingly, mind maps use an organic structure, usually centered on a large sheet of paper, with branches that radiate from the central topic. Use of illustrations and color appeal to the right side of the brain, which is normally neglected in traditional, linear note-taking approaches. The somewhat freewheeling format of mind maps facilitates problem solving by making it easier to visualize the "big picture." While this technique has benefits for everyone, a visual learner will especially appreciate mind maps.

One useful variation is to combine the organic structure of mind maps with traditional note-taking in a two-column format. This format is useful when taking notes in real time; it allows the note taker to spontaneously jot down points and related ideas during the course of the lecture or presentation.

Rules for creating mind maps:

- ❖ Put the main ideas in the middle of the sheet of paper and box it in.
- ❖ Add a branch from the center for each key point.
- ❖ Use a different color for each branch.
- ❖ Write one key word or short phrase on each branch and keep building out.
- ❖ Use arrows to show connections between branches.
- ❖ Use symbols or illustrations.
- ❖ Use CAPITAL letters.
- ❖ Let the size of the ideas reflect their relative importance.
- ❖ Use underlines and bold letters.
- ❖ Make it personal!
- ❖ Be creative!

Exhibit 2.1 "The World of Wine" Mind Map by Sandi Hotchkiss

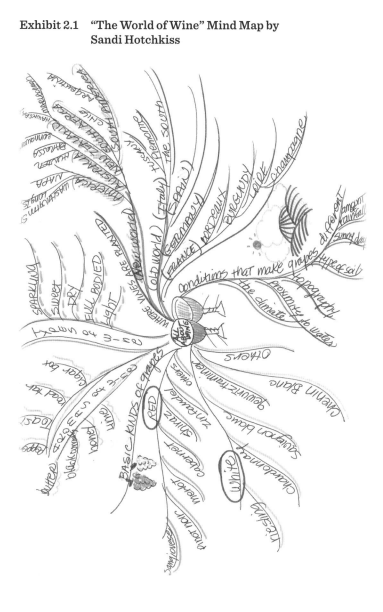

Exhibit 2.2 "Happiness" Mind Map by Paul Foreman

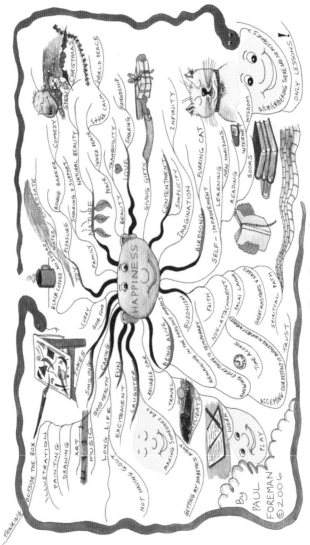

www.illustration.moonfruit.com

Devil's Advocate Technique

Tip #5: The devil's advocate technique imposes objectivity and compels divergent thinking.

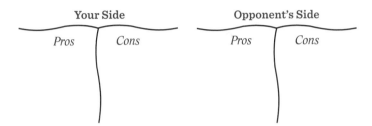

Your Side		Opponent's Side	
Pros	*Cons*	*Pros*	*Cons*

Definition: Devil's advocate—a person who advocates an opposing or unpopular cause for the sake of argument or to expose it to a thorough examination.

The devil's advocate technique forces us to consider the merits of the "other side" of an issue or topic. What we actually do is act as if we believe our opponent's side is right! In this way, we can gain a greater degree of objectivity. This technique is excellent for use in negotiations because it forces us to understand the other party's position and leads to a more realistic, effective bargaining process.

Consider that you are an analyst working at a leading market research firm. Your objective is to write a report on the market economics for product A. You have a strong idea that the market for product A is becoming more price-sensitive, and that the greater variations in price observed in the market are due to widening differences in product quality and branding (or perceptions of that product's quality or brand strength). You need to confirm your suspicion, and you're off to an interview with the marketing director of a major company who is responsible for marketing product A. But wait! If you and other analysts hold a similar view then you risk simply confirming something you already believe. Play the devil's advocate. Go into the meeting and ask questions designed to "disconfirm" what you think is true. You might ask, "So, is it true that the market for product A is becoming less price-sensitive?" The responses elicited may be essential to gaining a more complete understanding of the situation.

Idea Killers and Idea Growers

> **Tip #6:** Not challenging the obvious, evaluating ideas too quickly, and fear of looking the fool—these are the three greatest creativity inhibitors.

NOT CHALLENGING THE OBVIOUS

Creativity may suffer whenever we, as individuals, accept the status quo. We have to challenge the obvious. "Does one plus one really equal two?" It could indeed equal two. But it might equal eleven, as in "1 + 1 = 11." Or it could equate to "T," the result of placing one bar on top of the other.

Management consultants are constantly faced with the need to challenge the obvious. For instance, a client calls the consultant in and says, "Profitability is down because product costs are too high. Can you help me find a way to reduce them?" The consultant will instinctively challenge the obvious, asking whether it is the case that costs are too high. Perhaps it is another factor in the profitability mix (i.e., price or unit sales) that is really to blame.

EVALUATING IDEAS TOO QUICKLY

One way of confronting this barrier is to look at your hands. Think of your right hand as representing "idea production" and your left hand as representing "idea evaluation." Often an idea produced is immediately evaluated and possibly killed, e.g., by the phrase, "That won't work."

Success in creative thinking demands that the two hands should be separated, and that the left hand (idea evaluator) should be put to one side for the moment.

All ideas are acceptable in a creative situation, regardless of the quality. They may be good, bad, useful, useless, legal, illegal—it doesn't matter. Subsequently, the evaluation hand is brought back, and at that stage, a strange thing happens. Some of the ideas that originally would have been dismissed are looked at afresh, possibly with the comment: "Wait a minute, there may be something in that idea after all."

FEAR OF LOOKING THE FOOL

Failing to challenge the obvious and evaluating ideas too quickly may well be the by-products of being afraid to look like a fool. We learn to fear ridicule from an early age, and it follows us into later life. Many excellent examples are found in the world of management. In a hierarchical organization, junior team members are less likely to put forth wild, wacky ideas for fear that more senior team members will see them as silly. The junior does not want to destroy his or her chances of promotion, and therefore sticks to well-tried, analytical routines. At the other end of the scale, the most senior manager seeks to protect his or her image—one that has been built up over many years. That senior manager doesn't want to confirm to his or her underlings that he or she is a silly old fool. As a consequence, he or she does not propose any wild ideas either.

In short, we must fight apathy, hastiness, and insecurity. History abounds with instances of people who haven't been proactive enough in evaluating new ideas or who have been overly dismissive of new inventions or artistic or literary styles. This is particularly true where individuals are deemed authorities in their fields and err on the side of protecting their reputations. Here are several examples taken from the domain of science and art.

- ❖ Walt Disney was fired by an editor at the *Kansas City Star* newspaper because "he lacked imagination and had no good ideas." Years later, the Disney company bought ABC, which owned the *Kansas City Star*.

❖ Although Vincent van Gogh produced some 800 paintings, he was able to sell only one painting during his lifetime. *The Red Vineyard at Arles* was sold to the sister of one of his friends for 400 francs (approximately $50).

❖ In 1921, Newton Baker, U.S. Secretary of War, reacted to Brigadier General Billy Mitchell's claim that airplanes could sink battleships by dropping bombs on them: "That idea is so damned nonsensical and impossible that I'm willing to stand on the bridge of a battleship while that nitwit tries to hit it from the air."

❖ "Can't act. Can't sing. Can dance a little." MGM summary of a screen test of some guy named Fred Astaire, 1928.

❖ A Paris art dealer refused Pablo Picasso shelter when he asked if he could bring his paintings in from the rain.

❖ "I have traveled the length and breadth of this country and talked with the best people, and I can assure you that data processing is a fad that won't last out the year." The editor in charge of business books for Prentice Hall, 1957.

❖ "We don't like their sound and guitar music is on the way out." Decca Recording Co. on rejecting the Beatles, 1962.

❖ "But what. . .is it good for?" Engineer at IBM's Advanced Computing Systems Division, 1968, commenting on the microchip.

❖ Madonna, the best-selling female rock artist of the 20th century, was rejected by several music labels in the early 1980s. One talent agent is reputed to have said that her voice wasn't unique enough to stand out in a crowded marketplace.

❖ In the early 1990s, J.K. Rowling's *Harry Potter and the Philosopher's Stone* was rejected by more than a dozen UK publishers, the majority of which believed that the story wasn't mainstream enough.

The process of making mistakes in judgment and/or missing opportunities can be further illustrated within the framework of Type I and Type II errors. These two types of errors also are discussed within the topic of Hypothesis Testing in *Chapter 3*.

Type I errors are really errors of commission, while Type II errors are errors of omission. Type I errors are the result of projects that we should have rejected but instead adopted. Type II errors are the result of projects that we should have adopted but instead neglected. Type I errors result in observable failures. Type II errors result in missed opportunities.

A Type I error occurs when we take an action and it turns out to be a mistake. For example, whenever a top movie executive "green-lights" (okays) a movie project that turns out to be a failure, a Type I error is committed. The executive's career could suffer in a very public way, as these kinds of errors are very visible.

A Type II error occurs when we don't take an action, and the mistake comes from missing an opportunity. If one movie executive passes on a decision to make a movie, and another movie house later produces it, turning it into a blockbuster, a Type II error is committed.

Type II errors are often hard to see, even if they are common. The problem is that most Type II errors are never discovered. This is because many opportunities never immediately resurface. Projects or ideas, once killed or shelved, seldom get a second opinion. They are stopped without being shown to other people (or organizations) to see if someone else wants to take on the risk to pursue them.

Because Type II errors are mostly invisible, they come at less initial cost to people and organizations than do Type I errors. It's often easier to say no to something that might be a huge success than it is to say yes, because most of the time, no one will ever know what the outcome might have been. As long as most individuals (and the departments or organizations they work for) are evaluated based on the outcomes of their decisions, and not on what opportunities they might have missed, Type II errors will never be fully monetized.

Tip #7: Keep a mental list of idea "killers" and idea "growers."

Idea Killers

We tried it before.   *It would cost too much.*

That's not my job.

That's not your job.   *That's not how we do it.*

Why don't you put that in writing?   *It's impossible.*

That sounds crazy to me.

You may be right, but...   *Maybe next year.*

If it ain't broke, don't fix it.

It would take too much time.

Our customer would never go for that.

I don't think that's important.

My mind is definitely made up.

Our company is too small.

It's good enough.   *Our company is too big.*

That's a stupid idea.   *We don't have time right now.*

I don't need any more information.

You can't do that here.

Idea Growers

Are there any questions?

*Before we make a final decision,
let's review all the options.*

*Where else can we go for additional
information on that?*

May I ask a question? *What would happen if…?*

*In light of the new information,
I've changed my mind.*

How could we improve…?

I'd like to get your help with an idea I'm working on.

Let me ask you for some ideas on…

Is this what you meant?

Who else would be affected?

What have we missed?

Why do we always do it like that?

Wouldn't it be fun if…?

What ideas have you come up with?

How many ways could we…?

Thank you!

Brainstorming

Tip #8: Brainstorming has rules: quantity of ideas is preferred, wacky ideas are welcomed, delayed evaluation is mandatory, and "hitchhiking" is encouraged.

Ideas are the lifeblood of creativity, and brainstorming is a method to generate ideas. Brainstorming sessions are usually conducted in a group of between six and fifteen people. The setting is a room equipped with a whiteboard (or flip chart) so that ideas can be written down. The goal of brainstorming is to produce "novel but appropriate" ideas—the very heart of creativity. To achieve this goal, one must adhere to the "rules" of brainstorming.

First, quantity of ideas is the primary objective. Ideas should flow right from participants' tongues to the whiteboard. Second, to get people to come up with truly novel ideas, we say "wackier is better." Let the ideas flow by themselves. No one should fear looking the fool. All ideas, however wild or silly, are accepted. Third, delayed evaluation is mandatory. It is contradictory to try to create ideas and evaluate them at the same time. Any such attempt will curtail the creative process.

Fourth, as the session progresses, people will naturally "hitchhike" on ideas. "Oh that idea reminds of this" and "If that is so, then how about. . ." Hitchhiking means that one person is able to use another person's idea to go further and supply another idea. Toward the end of the brainstorming session, ideas will be scattered haphazardly from one end of the whiteboard to the other. This is perfectly natural. This may cause some participants to giggle or burst out laughing because very rarely does anyone experience this kind of free-flowing activity, especially in an office environment. Once ideas are regrouped and summarized, the results may be truly surprising. Managers, for example, who are unfamiliar with the power of brainstorming sessions are typically amazed at how many commercially viable ideas, that have never been previously uncovered, exist in the "collective mind" of their staff members and employees.

Business Brainstorming Questionnaire

The business questionnaire per **Exhibit 2.3** is a deceptively thought-provoking tool for increasing your understanding of your company, its products, and the current market opportunities. It yields the best results if completed as a group brainstorming session, which can take place on company premises.

This questionnaire includes a most intriguing question: "What business are we *really* in?" Participants' responses to this question may help a company redefine its business by enlarging its scope (or sometimes by narrowing it). Many business leaders have used this question to find new market opportunities. Too often, the business we believe we are in has been too narrowly defined or has become narrowed over the passage of time. Consider a company that prints newspapers. What business are they in? The likely answer is "the newspaper business." But what business are they really in? A possible answer is "the information business." Such a newly defined business scope conjures up new possibilities.

The opportunity faced by such a company may be the challenge, not of selling more newspapers, but rather of entering new but related markets. Is an airline company in the airline business or the transportation business? How about Coca-Cola? Coke used to define itself as being in the carbonated soft drink market, where it enjoyed an 80 percent market share. When Coke redefined its market in terms of ready-to-drink beverages, its market share fell to 10 percent. The ready-to-drink beverage market includes bottled water, orange juice, milk, and any other drink sold in a bottle, can, or container. Such a redefinition radically altered the company's perception of its market potential, and led to reinvigorated marketing efforts.

Exhibit 2.3   What Business Are We *Really* In?

I. What is our business?

    1a. What business are we really in?

    1b. What business should we be in?

    1c. What business(es) are we in, but perhaps shouldn't be?

    1d. Where do we see ourselves in a year? Two years? Five years? Ten years? (And why?)

    1e. How will macroeconomic, political, and geopolitical changes affect our business?

II. Who are we?

    2a. Exercise: Create a one-page résumé for our company and include:

> Experience
> Education
> Accomplishments
> References

    2b. What are we really good at doing? (What are our core competencies?)

    2c. Ask yourself: What assets do or can I bring to our company? What skills? What contacts?

    2d. What things should we be good at (but aren't yet)?

III. What are we selling, to whom?

    3a. Who are our customers? Who buy(s) from our company? (Who buys each product?)

    3b. Why do they buy?

    3c. What are we really selling? What benefits are our customers buying?. . .receiving?

    3d. Who doesn't buy (but could or should)?

    3e. Why don't they?

IV. Who is our competition?

4a. Who competes with us? What business are they in?

4b. What are their unique selling points/advantages vis-à-vis our company?

4c. What are their weaknesses vis-à-vis our company?

4d. How do they advertise and promote?

4e. What are their pricing and discounting policies?

4f. What are their customer service policies and practices?

4g. Who are their key people? What do we know about them? Experience and qualifications? Strengths and weaknesses? Personality traits?

V. What is our competitive position?

5a. What markets are we in?

5b. Who is our competition (in each market)?

5c. How are we positioned against the competition?

5d. How or where are we stronger? How or where are we weaker?

5e. If we worked for a competitor, how would we go about attacking our company to steal our company's business?

VI. How can we improve customer service?

6a. How do our customers feel about our company's service? Why?

6b. Where is our service strong? What do people compliment us on, or thank us for?

6c. Where can we improve our service? What complaints have we had (even if they were not our fault)? How are complaints handled? Can this be improved?

6d. What customer service practices are established as our company's policies? Are they written down? Where? Does everyone know about them?

6e. How can we make our customers feel like "part of the team"?

6f. How many ways can you think of to offer better service and/or value to our customers? (At this stage, think of as many ideas as you can—quantity, not quality—for now, at least.)

VII. Advertising and Promotion

How many ways can you think of to promote our company's business? (At this stage, let your imagination run wild: wacky, impractical ideas are as welcome as practical ones. Again, quantity over quality: the list can be whittled down later.)

Reframing Problems

> **Tip #9:** Consider whether a problem is really the problem. Think in terms of redefining the problem.

Ponder the following problem: "A restaurant is losing customers because customers are annoyed at how long it takes to line up outside in order to get a seat inside the restaurant."

If you were hired as a consultant, reporting to the headquarters of the restaurant chain, what would you suggest?

Typical solutions to be anticipated include:

- ❖ Enlarging the restaurant facilities in order to serve more customers
- ❖ Streamlining the menu in order to make ordering and delivery of food faster
- ❖ Refusing to let customers occupy tables if not ordering food; no "drinking-only" tables

These are all potential solutions. Nevertheless, they address only one of a number of possible general objectives: to speed up the process of getting customers through the dining process. An alternative goal is to find ways to keep people from getting annoyed at lining up. This suggests a host of potential strategies, such as installing televisions that customers could watch while they wait for a table, giving them free snacks while they wait in line, conducting market research while they wait in line, or having live or videotaped entertainment (e.g., magicians) to amuse persons in the line.

Still another objective is to keep the restaurant from having too many customers at one particular time of day. One idea/strategy would be to get more of the regular restaurant customers to come at non-peak hours. This might be accomplished by giving special dinner or drink discounts during certain hours of the day or holding special promotional events, such as speaking engagements, book signings, and guitar solos.

It is rare for people to step back and try to define alternative goals. Instead, most people read or hear of a problem and almost immediately begin generating strategies. One way to become more creative is by explicitly defining a minimum of two or three different goals for each problem situation.

Here is another example: An agricultural importer's association was attempting to seek a way to reduce the number of bruised pears which occurred when these fruits were transported. The importers initially defined their goal as "decreasing the rate with which pears became bruised or damaged when shipped." This led to various strategies for modifying distribution systems and packing procedures, such as including more padding around the pears and using smaller packing boxes. Although all of these strategies provided partial solutions, none was considered a breakthrough.

Reframing the problem led to a new goal: "creating a pear that is less likely to be bruised!" This entailed hiring individuals to look into the process of breeding pears. By exploring strategies to modify the pear, a portion of the problem was eventually solved. An "apple-pear" was born—a fruit with some of a pear's taste but with an apple's sturdiness. Now grocery stores could be supplied with large quantities of unblemished pear hybrids. Get into the habit of asking if the problem really is the problem. Is the goal really the goal?

Selling Creative Ideas

Tip #10: In selling creative ideas, most people are moved more by the depth of a person's conviction and commitment than they are by the details of a logical presentation.

To turn any creative idea into an innovative reality, an individual must obtain the support of key persons in an organization. In reality, the acceptance of a creative idea will have as much or more to do with company politics as with technical considerations. First, think of everybody as being your ally. Get initial feedback from people lower in the organizational structure and use it as a trial session to see what questions people have and what weaknesses and strengths are attributed to your idea. Never think you can please everyone; there will always be objectors. In fact, one way to gather support for your project is to ask for input from those you expect will be most affected.

Note that most good ideas are defeated by irrelevant issues. It should come as no surprise that the people who are most affected by the potential implementation of an idea tend to have a knack for raising irrelevant issues. Use this fact to your advantage. Make note of such issues and prepare to defend against them.

Assuming your idea is good, people will want to invest in it. Let them. It is important to give the impression that you do not want to take total credit for the idea you have created. People who do invest in your idea will hope to get something in return. Upon their acceptance of your idea, you have to determine what that "something" is. Never believe that you will not have to alter your idea; compromise is an inevitable reality.

Last, think hard about your ultimate decision makers—your real audience—and do some research. The better you know who your audience is, the better you can tailor your presentation. The ultimate presentation is customized, organized, and passionate. Strive to combine logic and novelty, but remember, above all else, that research indicates that people are persuaded more by passion and dedication to an idea than they are by a logical, detailed presentation.

Chapter 3

Decision Making

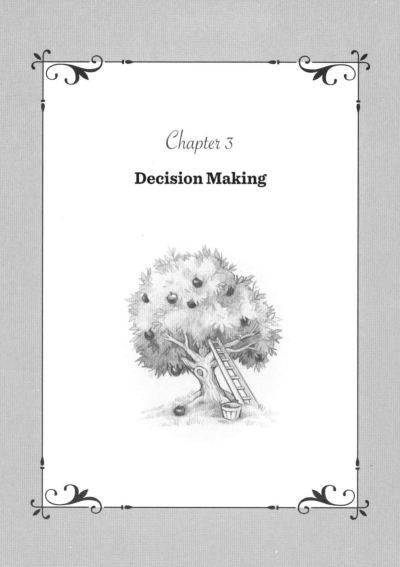

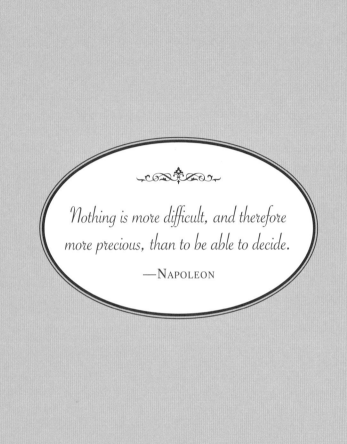

Nothing is more difficult, and therefore
more precious, than to be able to decide.

—NAPOLEON

Overview

This chapter introduces a variety of tools that can be used in making decisions for the purpose of solving problems or capturing opportunities. In this respect, it addresses applied reasoning. Perhaps the most important benefit of these techniques lies in our ability to use them to structure the thinking process. Imagine building a house without a plan! Adding structure to the decision-making process is like having a blueprint before building a house. Certainly a house could be built without a blueprint, but not as accurately or efficiently as it would be with one. A crucial distinction between structuring decisions and decision making is that structuring doesn't make decisions—people do.

The tools presented here are principally "trees" and "boxes." Trees impose order and hierarchy; boxes summarize data or information. Using trees is similar to flowcharting, and decision-event trees provide a classic example of techniques used to diagram information and to visualize outcomes.

Using boxes is similar to using a table to sort information or data, although in this material, "boxes" most often refers to matrixes. Frequently, the need exists to contrast information according to two (or more) variables, and this leads to four (or more) distinct outcomes. Work done in a factory might involve making small and large widgets and silver-colored and gold-colored widgets. Matrixes help us to set up the information in a table to quickly see how many items fall within each category: silver-colored widgets that are small, silver-colored widgets that are large, gold-colored widgets that are small, and gold-colored widgets that are large.

Weighted ranking is a technique to help us quantify the decision-making process in order to evaluate outcomes or options. We rank items and assign weights to them. An example occurs if we are buying a house and want to make the best decision. Say we believe, for example, that the ideal house is a combination of having the right location, size, and livability. By ranking prospective houses not only under each of the three categories, but by also assigning weights (or probabilities) to them, the optimal choice is quantifiable.

Hypothesis testing is useful when we want to test an idea or theory. It provides a framework for testing ideas and it begins with a hypothesis—a statement that we are trying to prove. Statements begin as questions and run the gamut of social science, business, or science: "Are green-eyed people more gregarious?" (social science); "Do stockbrokers really make better stock investment decisions than regular business people?" (business); "Do I have cancer?" (science).

Lastly, in examining the Prisoner's Dilemma, a mixed-motive game, we gain insights into the benefits of cooperation versus competition, specifically as they relate to individual versus group decisions.

Pros-and-Cons Analysis

Tip #11: Pros-and-cons analysis may be illustrated using a "T-Account," with pros on one side and cons on the other side.

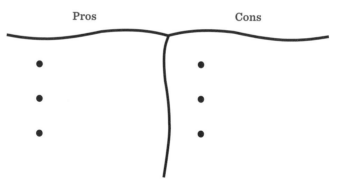

How many sides are there to every issue? Actually there are three. There are two distinct sides, as well as the "middle" view. But in pros-and-cons analysis, we assume, for simplicity, that there are two sides to every issue. The advantages are called "pros" and the disadvantages are called "cons." Our practical goal is to evaluate a topic or issue by generating three support points for each side prior to evaluation.

Seeing both sides of an issue is the cornerstone of a well-rounded thinking process. A secondary benefit of pros-and-cons analysis is that it forces us to consider positive points, not just negative ones. Most people are naturals at finding flaws! Pros-and-cons analysis brings balance. The benefits of high school or college debate is that it trains students to consider two sides of any issue. During a given tournament, a debater must be prepared to both defend and attack different sides of the same topic.

Note that pros-and-cons analysis should include both qualitative and quantitative support points, if applicable.

REPLACE A HISTORICAL BUILDING?

Imagine for a moment working as a professional for the urban planning department of a major city. As a staff member, you must make a recommendation on whether to replace a historical building located in the city's downtown center with a modern building. In order to engage all-around thinking—thinking that encompasses both sides of an issue—let's fill in the chart on the next page, placing support examples next to each bullet point.

Topic: "Although most people would agree that historical buildings represent a valuable record of any society's past, municipal governments should resolve doubt in favor of removing old buildings when such buildings stand on ground that planners feel could be better used."

Outline the likely pros and cons behind any decision to remove or keep a historical building.

Outline Template for Pros and Cons

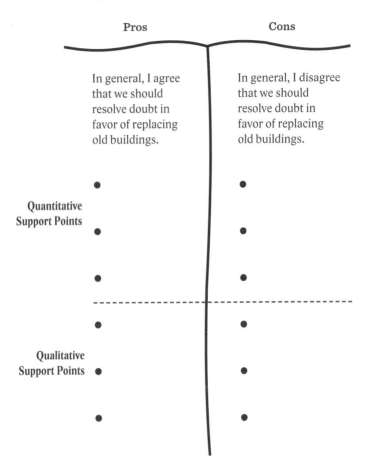

Pros   Cons

In general, I agree that we should resolve doubt in favor of replacing old buildings.

In general, I disagree that we should resolve doubt in favor of replacing old buildings.

Quantitative Support Points

Qualitative Support Points

Filling in the Pros and Cons

Pros	Cons
In general, I agree that we should resolve doubt in favor of replacing old buildings.	In general, I disagree that we should resolve doubt in favor of replacing old buildings.

Quantitative Support Points

Pros	Cons
• Revenue streams: New buildings earn more money in rent or sales.	• Revenue streams: Old buildings earn money from tourists.
• Revenue streams: New buildings earn more money in taxes.	• Revenue streams: Wealthy individuals often donate money to preserve old historical buildings.
• Costs: Old buildings have high maintenance costs which could be avoided if we built a new building.	• Costs: There is a huge capital outlay to begin construction on a new building which ties up valuable municipal funds.

Qualitative Support Points

Pros	Cons
• Safety: New buildings are safer.	• Educational: There is cultural, educational, and historical worth in old buildings.
• Architectural: New buildings are more visually harmonious with other modern buildings ("harmony in parity").	• Architectural: Old buildings offer an interesting visual contrast to modern buildings ("harmony in contrast").
• Aesthetics: New buildings are a sign of power and progress.	• Aesthetics: Old buildings bear a sense of nostalgia.

PROBLEM 6 CORPORATE TRAINING

One more! Fill in the chart on the following page with hypothetical but plausible support points to illustrate the pros and cons of providing on-site corporate training.

Topic: "The Head of the Human Resources Department of Super Corp. believes that a formal in-house training program is required to build employee skills in order for employees to perform new tasks and to avoid the costs associated with hiring for new positions from outside the company. Certain key executives, however, believe that formal in-house training will either take up valuable company time without proven effectiveness or be lost due to the high rate of employee turnover."

Using pros-and-cons analysis, evaluate the case for and against corporate in-house training.

Outline for Pros and Cons

	Pros	Cons
	Yes, I agree that we should provide in-house training.	No, I don't think we should provide in-house training.
	●	●
Quantitative Support Points	●	●
	●	●
- - - - - - - - - - - - - - - - - - -		
	●	●
Qualitative Support Points	●	●
	●	●

Matrixes

Tip #12: A matrix is a useful tool to summarize data that can be contrasted across two variables and sorted into four distinct outcomes.

UNDERSTANDING MATRIXES

The most common matrixes appear as two-column, two-row tables. A matrix is used to present data, where two items are being contrasted with two other items and there are four possibilities or outcomes. The matrix below is based on a famous time management principle highlighting the need to concentrate on "important but not urgent" tasks.

Exhibit 3.1 Time Management Matrix

	Important Tasks	*Unimportant Tasks*
Urgent Tasks	**Important and Urgent Tasks** • Example: A major project is due in three days! • Results in crisis management • Time management problems are not found here.	**Unimportant but Urgent Tasks** • Example: The phone rings and you need to pick it up (this is an unimportant but urgent task; it is not related to the project at hand). • Good time management means putting limits here.
Not Urgent Tasks	**Important but not Urgent Tasks** • Example: A major project is assigned but is not due for three months. • Never get around to it • Not enough time devoted here • Divides effective and ineffective individuals • Time management problems are found here.	**Unimportant and Not Urgent Tasks** • Example: You attend a community service event by day (unrelated to the project at hand); later that night you watch TV. • Busywork; tension-relieving work; wasted time • Low-priority items • Good time management means putting limits here.

Matrixes work with information, in addition to numbers, as long as information makes sense when read across as well as down. When matrixes contain numbers, our task is to fill in known information, and through simple mathematical deduction, find the unknown information.

Take for example a batch of toys, fresh off the production line. Each toy has exactly two of four characteristics: each is either blue or green and either large or small. A matrix must total across as well as down. This is the figure that appears in the bottom right-hand corner of the extended matrix, represented by three "xxx"s. The dotted lines are merely useful extensions of the original four-box matrix.

Toy Production
Here is the nine-box table used to set up this problem:

Color

		Blue	Green	
Size	**Large**	X	X	XX
	Small	X	X	XX
		XX	XX	XXX

Say we have a batch of 100 toys. The number 100 will be placed in the extended bottom right corner. Based on available data, the matrix might be filled in as follows:

Color

		Blue	Green	
	Large	20	45	65
Size	**Small**	10	25	35
		30	70	100

Why do matrixes work so neatly? Things work neatly as long as all data is "mutually exclusive and collectively exhaustive." What does this mean? *Mutually* exclusive is a fancy way of saying that the data does not overlap; it is distinct. In other words, toys must be either blue or green and either large or small. We can't have toys which are both blue and green (for example, colored blue-green or striped) or both large and small (that is, medium-sized). *Collectively exhaustive* means that the number of data is finite. There are exactly 100 toys, of which 30 are blue, 70 are green, 65 are large, and 35 are small. Data which is mutually exclusive and collectively exhaustive ensures that everything will total both "down" and "across." Matrixes also work with information (see **Exhibit 3.1**), in addition to numbers, as long as information makes sense when read across as well as down.

Because matrixes handle information so neatly, it is not surprising that they are a consultant's favorite presentation tool. Folklore has it that one junior management consultant became so enamored with matrixes that he called them "boxes of joy"!

The truth is that matrixes are wonderful tools that can encapsulate a great deal of information. Case in point: The following write-up sheds light on just how much information can be gleaned from The Lots-Little Matrix (**Exhibit 3.2**), which can be used to understand how the two basic components of a company's profitability—margin and volume—accelerate or trade-off with each another in a competitive business marketplace.

Exhibit 3.2   The Lots-Little Matrix

Margin

		High	Low
Volume	**High**	1. Lots (Q), Lots ($)	2. Lots (Q), Little ($)
	Low	3. Little (Q), Lots ($)	4. Little (Q), Little ($)

Notes:

(Q) = Volume = quantity of product sold (unit sales)

($) = Margin = dollar "profit" per unit of product sold

The Lots-Little Matrix is useful for pinpointing where specific companies or industries are competitively positioned:

1. **Sell a lot (Q), at a lot ($)**

   "Selling large quantities at high margins." The computer software industry has provided examples of companies (Apple and Microsoft in their early days) that are/were able to sell large volumes of product at high margins, within limited time frames.

2. **Sell a lot (Q), at a little ($)**

   "Selling large quantities at low margins." The airlines industry is known for selling large volumes of product (seats) at low margins.

3. **Sell a little (Q), at a lot ($)**

   "Selling small volumes at high margins." Companies within the fashion industry (haute couture) are known for being able to sell relatively smaller volumes of product at high margins (sometimes very high).

4. **Sell a little (Q), at a little ($)**

   "Selling small volumes at low margins." Sam's Fish & Chips (a generic, local food vendor) sells small volumes of product at low margins.

The Lots-Little Matrix helps tell a story about how businesses survive and thrive. Certainly companies would love to operate in category 1 and enjoy the best of both worlds: high volumes and high margins. But practically, the competitive marketplace does not usually allow such occurrences to be long lived. A company initially operating in category 1 would likely be forced into one of category 2 or 3, as a result of competitors entering their marketplace.

Many businesses operate in category 2 or 3. That is, they either have good volumes but lower margins (category 2) or lower volumes but good margins (category 3). Category 4 would invariably represent those small businesses that can sustain themselves, but are not able to grow to compete in categories 2 or 3. Generally, no major company within an established industry can sell only small volumes at low margins and survive for any extended time frame.

MATRIXES VS. TABLES

Confusion often arises regarding the use of tables and matrixes. While it is true that matrixes look like tables (actually, all matrixes are tables but not all tables are matrixes), they are distinctly different tools. As previously illustrated, matrixes must total across and down and do so because the data or information contained in them is mutually exclusive and collectively exhaustive. Tables simply display or group related information. However, tables should not be used to sort random data.

Table A works well because the information is related. Here, the study of marketing is displayed by breaking it down into four distinct areas.

Table A—The Marketing Mix

Product	Promotion
Price	Place (Distribution)

The information in **Table B** is not presented effectively because the words appear random and arbitrary.

Table B—Medical Discoveries in Europe

Paris	Madrid
London	Amsterdam

The cities mentioned above should, in all likelihood, be enumerated in a list:

1. Paris
2. London
3. Madrid
4. Amsterdam

Although **Exhibit 3.3** looks like a matrix, it is not one, because its information only "reads" down, but not across. The following write-up would likely accompany this chart:

> We hear so much about information today. But when is information deemed "good" information? Information is best understood by looking at it in terms of its four quality dimensions—accessible, summarized, relevant, and customized. When information touches all of these dimensions, it becomes both efficient and effective.
>
> The dimensions of "accessible" and "summarized" relate to the efficiency of information. The dimensions of "relevant" and "customized" relate to the effectiveness of information. The terms effective and efficient are, in casual conversation, often used interchangeably because information has traditionally been thought to be effective as soon as it has been deemed efficient—that is, when "accessible" (dimension 1) and "summarized" (dimension 2).
>
> It is the purpose of this chart to highlight the importance of effectiveness—"relevant" (dimension 3) and "customized" (dimension 4). Unless information is effective as well as efficient, it will not be easily adopted or internalized by the user. Without becoming effective, information cannot be easily recalled or acted upon. Information that has all four elements may be said to be "transparent." It is so ready and usable that it takes on the appearance of always being in the mind of the user.

Exhibit 3.3   The Effective Information Chart

	Dimension 1: "Accessible"	Dimension 3: "Relevant"	
E F F I C I E N C Y	Information must be constantly accessible and mobile. It can't be just stored in boxes. Key concept: readily locatable Catchwords: getable, findable	Information must be targeted and relevant so that it has meaning and significance to the user. Key concept: readily applicable Catchwords: targeted, applicable, pertinent	**E F F E C T I V E N E S S**
	Dimension 2: "Summarized"	**Dimension 4: "Customized"**	
	Information must be kept in summarized form. It must be distilled and condensed. Key concept: readily digestible Catchwords: compact, essential, distilled	Information must be able to be modified and tweaked to conform to the user's style or needs. Key concept: readily adaptable Catchwords: "ownable," styled, personalized	

USING MATRIXES

Job search: Of thirty-five applicants applying for a job, twenty had at least seven years' work experience, twenty-three had degrees, and three had less than seven years' work experience and did not have a degree. How many of the applicants had at least seven years' work experience and a degree?

Step #1: Sketch a matrix and enter given information into the appropriate boxes. The box containing the question mark depicts the value we're trying to find.

	< 7 years' work experience	≥ 7 years' work experience	
With degrees		?	23
No degrees	3		
		20	35

Step #2: Let's total the numbers on the side and bottom of the matrix, filling in the dotted boxes.

	< 7 years' work experience	≥ 7 years' work experience	
With degrees		?	23
No degrees	3		12
	15	20	35

Step #3: Since data must total down and across, we simply fill in remaining numbers within the middle four boxes.

	< 7 years' work experience	≥ 7 years' work experience	
With degrees	12	11	23
No degrees	3	9	12
	15	20	35

Eleven of the candidates, therefore, have at least seven years' work experience and hold degrees.

For each of the following problems, use matrix analysis to calculate the desired outcomes.

PROBLEM 7 SINGLES
In a graduate physics course, 70 percent of the students are male and 30 percent of the students are married. If 20 percent of the students are male and married, what percentage of female students are single?

PROBLEM 8 BATTERIES
For every batch of 100 batteries manufactured at a certain upstart factory, one-fifth of the batteries produced by the factory are defective and one-quarter of all batteries produced are rejected by the quality control technician. If one-tenth of the non-defective batteries are rejected by mistake, and if all the batteries not rejected are sold, then what percent of the batteries sold by the factory are defective?

Problem 9 Interrogation

Police who are trained in criminal interrogation techniques use questions to obtain information and evidence about the guilt or innocence of the subject being interrogated. There are four possible outcomes: (1) a person did commit a crime and is telling the truth (confessing to a crime they really did do); (2) a person did commit a crime and is not telling the truth (claiming to be innocent when they really did do it); (3) a person did not commit a crime and is telling the truth (claiming to be rightfully innocent for a crime they didn't do); and (4) a person did not commit a crime and is not telling the truth (confessing to a crime they actually didn't do).

Interrogators have past statistics to guide them. In short, police interrogators contend that when someone is accused of a crime and interrogation takes place, there is a 75 percent chance that a given person did not commit the crime, a 20 percent chance that a person is not telling the truth, and a 2 percent chance that a person will confess to a crime they didn't commit. Based on these statistics, what is the chance that a person actually committed the crime and is telling the truth (confessing to a crime they actually committed)?

Decision-Event Trees

> **Tip #13:** Decision-event trees are a way to represent graphically the multiple outcomes involved in a decision scenario.

Terms such as *felony*, *infraction*, *misdemeanor*, and *tort* are potentially very confusing for the layperson. How might a first-year law student put these words into a decision tree to help make sense out of case law? One idea would be to view each term in light of the severity of punishment that a court/jury could impose on a guilty verdict.

How are the following ten terms connected?

Felonies	*Civil Wrongs (private)*
Infractions	*Torts*
Homicide	*Treason*
Offenses	*Crimes (public)*
Misdemeanors	*Breach of Contract*

The decision-event tree per **Exhibit 3.4** acts as a flowchart to depict logical relationships among legal terms. Civil wrongs, also known as "private wrongs," occur between or among individuals. A breach of contract occurs when one party "breaks" a legal agreement. A tort is a general term used to describe acts that result in injury to another person (e.g., assault). Crimes, on the other hand, involve the state (public). Informally speaking, infractions are "minor offenses" (e.g., parking violations), misdemeanors are "minor criminal offenses" (e.g., shoplifting), and felonies are "major criminal offenses," of which homicide (murder) and treason are considered the most serious offenses.

Understandably, the above paragraph is difficult to read. We need a visual representation to summarize the type of crime and the severity of crime. Refer to **Exhibit 3.4** on page 74.

Exhibit 3.4   Decision-Event Tree—Legal Offenses

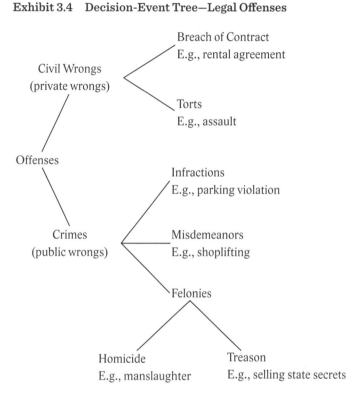

Breach of Contract
E.g., rental agreement

Civil Wrongs
(private wrongs)

Torts
E.g., assault

Offenses

Infractions
E.g., parking violation

Crimes
(public wrongs)

Misdemeanors
E.g., shoplifting

Felonies

Homicide
E.g., manslaughter

Treason
E.g., selling state secrets

Exhibit 3.5 provides an example of a decision-event tree showing the outcomes associated with tossing a coin three times? There are eight possibilities when a coin is tossed three times: Heads-Heads-Heads (HHH), Heads-Heads-Tails (HHT), Heads-Tails-Heads (HTH), Heads-Tails-Tails (HTT), Tails-Heads-Heads (THH), Tails-Heads-Tails (THT), Tails-Tails-Heads (TTH), and Tails-Tails-Tails (TTT). Even though writing out the possibilities using abbreviated letters is compact, it is not as easy to grasp until supplemented with a visual format. Decision-event trees are notably user-friendly.

Exhibit 3.5   Decision-Event Tree—Coin Tosses

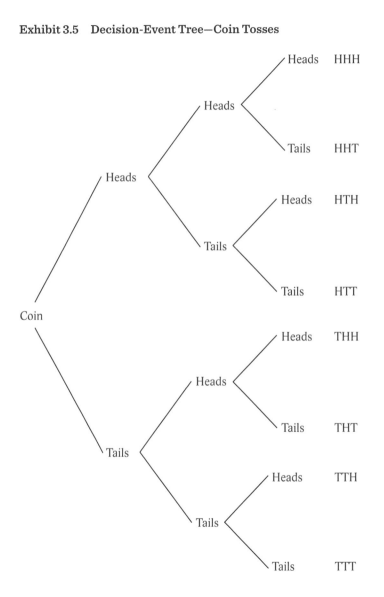

Exhibit 3.6 Probability Tree—Coin Tosses

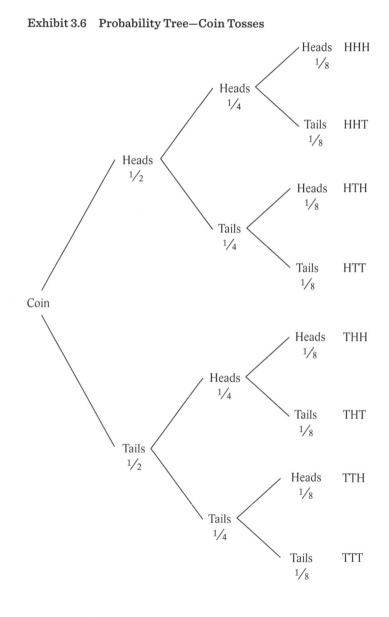

PROBLEM 10   SET MENU

A restaurant offers a set lunch menu. Diners have the choice of choosing between one of two appetizers (soup or salad), one of three main courses (pasta, chicken, or fish), one of two desserts (pie or cake), as well as coffee or tea. Draw a decision tree showing the total number of ways a diner can choose his or her meal.

Probability Trees

> **Tip #14:** The end branches of a probability tree must total to 1, which is equal to the aggregate of all individual probabilities.

Exhibit 3.6 illustrates the probabilities associated with each event. Note that probabilities always total to 1, if we add the probabilities at the endpoints (i.e., $8 \times \frac{1}{8} = 1.0$). Each endpoint equals $\frac{1}{8}$, which is the resultant probability of three consecutive tosses of a coin (i.e., $\frac{1}{2} \times \frac{1}{2} \times \frac{1}{2} = \frac{1}{8}$).

Weighted Ranking

> **Tip #15:** Weighted ranking is a tool for finding solutions using a weighted average. To calculate weighted average, we multiply each event by its associated weight and total the results. In the case of probabilities, we multiply each event by its respective probability and total the results.

Snapshot

The weighted average concept is actually quite intuitive. To find a weighted average, we multiply events by their respective weight and total the results. Events are the things that we wish to rate, rank, or judge. Weights refer to the amount of emphasis we want to attribute to each event and are commonly expressed as percentages, fractions, decimals, or probabilities. The beauty of weighted average is that we can assign different weights based on the relative importance of events—the more important the event, the more weight it is given.

Below is the weighted average formula for two events:

Weighted Average = (Event$_1$ × Weight$_1$) + (Event$_2$ × Weight$_2$)

An alternative format is:

Event$_1$ × Weight$_1$ = xx
Event$_2$ × Weight$_2$ = $\underline{\text{xx}}$
$\underline{\underline{\text{xx}}}$

Exam Time

A student scores 60 out of 100 points on his midterm exam and 90 out of 100 points on his final exam. If the exams are both weighted equally, counting for 50 percent of the student's final course grade, then what is his course grade?

60 × 50% = 30
90 × 50% = $\underline{45}$
$\underline{\underline{75}}$

Based on the same information above, what is the student's final course grade if the midterm exam is weighted 40 percent and the final exam is weighted 60 percent?

60 × 40% = 30
90 × 60% = $\underline{54}$
$\underline{\underline{78}}$

Note that the weights above could also be expressed using fractions or decimals:

$$60 \times \frac{40}{100} = 24$$

$$60 \times \frac{60}{100} = \underline{54}$$
$$\phantom{60 \times \frac{60}{100} = } \underline{\underline{78}}$$

$$60 \times 0.4 = 24$$
$$90 \times 0.6 = \underline{54}$$
$$ \underline{\underline{78}}$$

Hiring and promotion decisions are classic examples of situations in which subjective influences can override an objective decision-making process. Weighted ranking therefore presents a method to quantify decision opportunities.

Consider a company with ten salespersons, one of whom is to be named National Sales Manager. As depicted in **Exhibit 3.7**, the ten candidates are first ranked from 1 to 10 (10 being the highest rating) across three criteria.

The three criteria—technical skills, people skills, and track record—are weighted using the weights of 0.2, 0.3, and 0.5, respectively (see **Exhibit 3.8**). Note that instead of using decimals (0.2, 0.3, 0.5), we could also use percents (i.e., 20%, 30%, 50%), fractions (i.e., $^2/_{10}$, $^3/_{10}$, $^5/_{10}$), or even whole numbers such as 2, 3, and 5. Based on the results from weighting the data (per **Exhibit 3.9**), Sabrina receives the highest ranking while George gets the next highest ranking.

The weights used will typically add up to 1 or 100 percent, as is the case when dealing with percentages, fractions, decimals, or probabilities. Sometimes problems will use arbitrary weights that are not equal to 1.

Exhibit 3.7   Performance of Salespersons

	Technical skills and product knowledge	People skills and ability to communicate	Track record and ability to get things done
Albert	2	3	7
Betty	5	2	6
George	6	5	9
Jed	3	7	1
Jono	8	10	3
Martha	10	1	2
Patricia	1	4	8
Randy	9	9	4
Sabrina	4	6	10
William	7	8	5

Exhibit 3.8 Performance Using Weighted Average

	Technical skills and product knowledge Weight = 0.2	People skills and ability to communicate Weight = 0.3	Track record and ability to get things done Weight = 0.5	Total
Albert	$2 \times 0.2 = 0.4$	$3 \times 0.3 = 0.9$	$7 \times 0.5 = 3.5$	4.8
Betty	$5 \times 0.2 = 1.0$	$2 \times 0.3 = 0.6$	$6 \times 0.5 = 3.0$	4.6
George	$6 \times 0.2 = 1.2$	$5 \times 0.3 = 1.5$	$9 \times 0.5 = 4.5$	7.2
Jed	$3 \times 0.2 = 0.6$	$7 \times 0.3 = 2.1$	$1 \times 0.5 = 0.5$	3.2
Jono	$8 \times 0.2 = 1.6$	$10 \times 0.3 = 3.0$	$3 \times 0.5 = 1.5$	6.1
Martha	$10 \times 0.2 = 2.0$	$1 \times 0.3 = 0.3$	$2 \times 0.5 = 1.0$	3.3
Patricia	$1 \times 0.2 = 0.2$	$4 \times 0.3 = 1.2$	$8 \times 0.5 = 4.0$	5.4
Randy	$9 \times 0.2 = 1.8$	$9 \times 0.3 = 2.7$	$4 \times 0.5 = 2.0$	6.5
Sabrina	$4 \times 0.2 = 0.8$	$6 \times 0.3 = 1.8$	$10 \times 0.5 = 5.0$	7.6
William	$7 \times 0.2 = 1.4$	$8 \times 0.3 = 2.4$	$5 \times 0.5 = 2.5$	6.3

Exhibit 3.9 Ranking of Salespersons

	Technical skills and product knowledge Weight = 0.2	People skills and ability to communicate Weight = 0.3	Track record and ability to get things done Weight = 0.5	Total votes (The higher the better)	Rank (The lower the better)
Sabrina	$4 \times 0.2 = 0.8$	$6 \times 0.3 = 1.8$	$10 \times 0.5 = 5.0$	7.6	1
George	$6 \times 0.2 = 1.2$	$5 \times 0.3 = 1.5$	$9 \times 0.5 = 4.5$	7.2	2
Randy	$9 \times 0.2 = 1.8$	$9 \times 0.3 = 2.7$	$4 \times 0.5 = 2.0$	6.5	3
William	$7 \times 0.2 = 1.4$	$8 \times 0.3 = 2.4$	$5 \times 0.5 = 2.5$	6.3	4
Jono	$8 \times 0.2 = 1.6$	$10 \times 0.3 = 3.0$	$3 \times 0.5 = 1.5$	6.1	5
Patricia	$1 \times 0.2 = 0.2$	$4 \times 0.3 = 1.2$	$8 \times 0.5 = 4.0$	5.4	6
Albert	$2 \times 0.2 = 0.4$	$3 \times 0.3 = 0.9$	$7 \times 0.5 = 3.5$	4.8	7
Betty	$5 \times 0.2 = 1.0$	$2 \times 0.3 = 0.6$	$6 \times 0.5 = 3.0$	4.6	8
Martha	$10 \times 0.2 = 2.0$	$1 \times 0.3 = 0.3$	$2 \times 0.5 = 1.0$	3.3	9
Jed	$3 \times 0.2 = 0.6$	$7 \times 0.3 = 2.1$	$1 \times 0.5 = 0.5$	3.2	10

Chess

In chess, a pawn is worth one point, a knight or bishop is worth three points, a rook is worth five points, and a queen is worth nine points. Player A has two rooks, a knight, and three pawns. Player B has a bishop, four pawns, and a queen. Who is ahead and by how much?

	Player A	**Player B**
Pawns:	$3 \times 1 = 3$ pts	$4 \times 1 = 4$ pts
Bishops:		$1 \times 3 = 3$ pts
Knights:	$1 \times 3 = 3$ pts	
Rooks:	$2 \times 5 = 10$ pts	
Queens:		$1 \times 9 = 9$ pts
	16 points	16 points

Answer: Both players are tied at 16 points each.

Sweet Sixteen

On her sixteenth birthday, Jane received $500 from each of her two uncles. Both amounts had been deposited in two local banks, one bank paying 6 percent per annum and the other paying 7 percent per annum. How much in total did she earn from these two investments over the course of exactly one year?

$$\$500 \times 6\% = \$30$$
$$\$500 \times 7\% = \underline{\$35}$$
$$\underline{\underline{\$65}}$$

PROBLEM 11   INVESTOR

An investor is looking at three different investment possibilities. The first investment opportunity has a $\frac{1}{6}$ chance of returning $90,000, a $\frac{1}{2}$ chance of returning $50,000, and a $\frac{1}{3}$ chance of losing $60,000. A second investment opportunity has a $\frac{1}{2}$ chance of returning $100,000 and a $\frac{1}{2}$ chance of losing $50,000. The third investment opportunity has a $\frac{1}{4}$ chance of returning $100,000, a $\frac{1}{4}$ chance of returning $60,000, a $\frac{1}{4}$ chance of losing $40,000, and a $\frac{1}{4}$ chance of losing $80,000. Assuming the investor chooses to invest in all three investments, what will be his or her expected return?

Utility Analysis

> **Tip #16:** Utility analysis takes into account desirability of outcomes, which may be different from monetary payoffs.

Utility is "desirability." Utility analysis is useful in those situations in which we seek to match utility with probability. In other words, these two terms must be distinguished at the outset. Utility is "what we want"; probability is "what we get."

Consider for a moment the dilemma of a fourth-year college student who is trying to decide what to do with his or her future. The student knows that he or she wants to do one of three things: pursue work as a travel writer, join the diplomatic service, or go into business and work as a sales representative. In terms of how rewarding these experiences would be, the student believes that pursuing work as a travel writer is to be rated first, joining the diplomatic service is to be rated second, and going into business is to be rated third. But how do we assign a value to the desirability of these options? Money will not be an appropriate utility because the person is likely not thinking in terms of how much money can be earned, but rather how much he or she would like to pursue each of these options. The world might be our "oyster," but how do we evaluate our options? Expected Value (EV) is defined as the product (multiplication) of a given utility and its corresponding probability.

	Utility		Probability		EV
Work as travel writer	100	×	0.10	=	10
Join diplomatic corps	70	×	0.40	=	28
Go into business	40	×	0.50	=	20

Note that the probabilities assigned incorporate the risk and/or skill level required to pursue each option. According to the above analysis, "Join the diplomatic service" provides the greatest Expected Value (EV) and, objectively, this option should be chosen.

The following rules can be used to choose values for utilities. Always pick a value of 100 for the most desirable (non-monetary) outcome. This provides an analytical boundary and makes choosing other values easier. In reality, "Work as a travel writer" might be less than 100. A "100" might represent a dream scenario in which a person wins the lottery and retires to a deserted island to paint sunsets. This is not shown as an option owing to the incredibly low probability associated with it. One more rule is to make each utility a multiple of 10 (i.e., 10, 20, 70, 100), for any more precision would be suspect.

Of course, utility could still be calculated in terms of money. Utility measured in monetary terms is the focus of our next problem. Four teams have made the semi-finals of the NBA Championships. It is time to place a bet.

If there were costs associated with the opportunity to place a bet, then we would have to subtract this cost from our Expected Value in order to arrive at our price. However, such a fixed cost would not affect the result of our Utility Analysis. The team with the highest Expected Value would be the best bet.

In the summary that follows, we see that option 1 has the highest probability and option 4 has the highest payoff (utility), but neither results in the highest expected value (EV). It turns out that placing a bet for team 2 or team 3 leads to the highest expected value (EV). This is because expected payoff must be tempered with probability of the outcome. The analysis below helps us see the optimal outcomes quickly.

(Bet) Option	**Outcome**	**Utility**		**Probability**		**EV**
Team 1	$200	×	0.50	=	$100
Option 1	Team 2	$0	×	0.20	=	$0
Team 3	$0	×	0.20	=	$0
Team 4	$0	×	0.10	=	$0
					$100
Team 1	$0	×	0.50	=	$50
Option 2	Team 2	$600	×	0.20	=	$120
Team 3	$0	×	0.20	=	$0
Team 4	$0	×	0.10	=	$0
					$120
Team 1	$0	×	0.50	=	$0
Option 3	Team 2	$0	×	0.20	=	$0
Team 3	$600	×	0.20	=	$120
Team 4	$0	×	0.10	=	$0
					$120
Team 1	$0	×	0.50	=	$0
Option 4	Team 2	$0	×	0.20	=	$0
Team 3	$0	×	0.20	=	$0
Team 4	$900	×	0.10	=	$90
					$100

Sunk Costs

Tip #17: Sunk costs are irrelevant to future decision making.

Suppose you bought a discounted, nonrefundable plane ticket for $500, which you had planned to use when going on vacation.

No sooner had you bought the ticket did an important meeting arise, one that you had been waiting months to arrange. It could definitely help move your career forward. You have a dilemma. How do you decide in a logical way what to do? Do you use the plane ticket you paid good money for or forfeit it and attend the important meeting?

According to economic theory, any past costs, also known as sunk costs, have no effect on future decision making. The only thing that affects future decisions are the costs and benefits of the two (or more) alternative courses of action. The cost of the plane ticket is considered a sunk cost and has no effect on the decision to go on vacation or attend the meeting.

This means that if the net benefits of this meeting are deemed greater than the net benefits of attending this trip, then we forget about the trip and attend the meeting. Of course, we must factor in both costs and benefits. The benefits of attending the meeting might involve securing a large account, getting promoted, or perhaps finding out about a new job opportunity. The costs involved might include travel to the meeting and/or the time and effort needed to prepare for the meeting. The benefits of going on vacation may well involve having a relaxing, rejuvenating experience. The costs will include accommodation and personal expenses incurred while on vacation.

From a rational perspective, it makes perfect sense to ignore sunk costs. But from an emotional standpoint, it may be very difficult to do so. We may view sunk costs as "wasted" costs and instinctively want to "save" them by investing more time and money in the project or undertaking. We've all heard of the saying "to throw good money after bad," and perhaps the telltale sign of the sunk cost dilemma is encapsulated by the words: "Just think how much time and money we've already spent." The fact that we have spent time and money on a particular project or undertaking, which may have resulted in that project getting closer to completion, may in itself make continuing work on that project a favorable course of action. However, the costs so far incurred are irrelevant to the future decision on whether to continue working on it or abandon it and change course.

It is especially difficult to detach ourselves emotionally from personal projects that have become "labors of love." We must, however, at least acknowledge, that rationally, our previous time, effort, and money act as a sunk cost. In order to break our emotional attachment to sunk costs for the purpose of making an objective decision and possibly changing course, it is important to consider three things:

1) Recognize that cutting your losses does not necessarily mean you've made a mistake because your decision to pursue the original course of action may have been the smartest course of action at that time.

2) Enlist a few people you trust and ask them for their opinion. A person viewing our situation as an outsider may have a much more objective view of our situation.

3) Realize that most situations carry with them the seeds of greater benefit. Knowledge, skills, and insights gained from previous experiences can be applied to new situations moving forward.

Hypothesis Testing

Tip #18: For the purposes of hypothesis testing, the minimum requirement for causal inference is evaluation using a "two-way" table.

It is not uncommon to try to evaluate claims that have yet to be proven. This is the basis of hypothesis testing. Although hypothesis testing is usually associated with hard-core research, it also has wide-ranging applications and can be used to try to determine answers to the following everyday questions: Do vegetarians live longer? Does TV viewing lead to violence? Does a new miracle headache drug work better than aspirin? Do stockbrokers make better stock market investment decisions than regular business people? Do I have cancer?

Invariably, we end up asking whether one thing leads to another, and this brings cause and effect into play. The minimum requirement for causal inference is evaluation using a "two-way" table. This "two-way" table is a de facto matrix, used to contrast information according to two variables, and for which information can be divided into four categories.

Consider whether a greater than average job skill level leads to a greater than average annual income level.

Job Skill Level

		Higher	Lower	
Annual Salary	**Higher**	30	20	50
	Lower	20	30	50
		50	50	100

In the previous chart, let's assume exactly 100 persons were surveyed. This cross-tabulation, which is fictitious though not implausible, suggests that there is a relationship between a person's job skill level and his or her annual income level. After all, more than half of those individuals with lower levels of job skill also have lower levels of annual job income. That is, 30 individuals are represented by the box where "lower meets lower." Likewise, more than half of those individuals with higher levels of job skill also have higher levels of annual job income. Note that there are 30 individuals represented by the box where "higher meets higher."

Consider, on the other hand, what we would expect to see if there were no apparent relationship between job skill levels and annual income levels. Indeed, we would expect to see a proportionate number of people in each sub-category. In fact, assuming that people were chosen at random, we would expect to see exactly twenty-five persons in each sub-category.

Job Skill Level

		Higher	Lower	
Annual Salary	Higher	25	25	50
	Lower	25	25	50
		50	50	100

Stockbroker Endorsement

> "My broker helped me achieve an above-average return on my stock investment portfolio. His predictions turned out to be correct, whether judging the stock market index or the performance of individual companies. My friend, a seasoned businessperson, tried to predict the market himself and consistently achieved a negative return. The advice is clear. Keep your hand out of the cookie jar and don't try to predict the stock market yourself. Use a broker and get the returns you deserve."

How do you go about evaluating the more general claim that brokers do in fact make better stock market investment decisions than do "regular" businesspersons? In testing this hypothesis, we also employ a method based on experimental design, which utilizes a matrix consisting of two primary rows and two primary columns, with nine boxes of numerical data.

	Correct Predictions	Incorrect Predictions	Total Number of Predictions	
Stock Brokers	50	150	200	25.0%
Regular Business-persons	100	700	800	12.5%
	150	850	1,000	

Note that in this hypothetical example, percentage calculations are required because the actual numbers of predictions are of unequal size (predictions by stockbrokers total 200, while predictions by regular businesspersons total 800). The percentage of correct predictions is calculated as follows: stockbrokers: $50/200 = 25\%$; regular businesspersons: $100/800 = 12.5\%$.

The numbers in the chart above are hypothetical. However, based on these numbers (and sidestepping further statistical analysis for simplicity's sake), we find that brokers are twice as likely to make correct predictions (25% vs. 12.5%), and we can conclude that there is merit in the ability of brokers, as compared with regular businesspersons, to make accurate stock market predictions. It is especially important to think not just in terms of the number of correct predictions made, but of the percentage of correct predictions made over both categories (i.e., the percentage of correct predictions made by stockbrokers versus the percentage of correct predictions made by regular businesspersons). For a comparative problem, refer to *Shark*, page 129.

Hypothesis testing is about making predictions. By the word "hypothesis," we mean "a statement yet to be proven." For example, let us say we are on our way to the doctor's office for a major checkup.

In particular, we are concerned about the possibility that we might have cancer, but we know it is a rather unlikely occurrence. So we enter our checkup with the hypothesis: "I do not have cancer."

Upon completion of tests, we will be diagnosed either as having cancer or not. In reality, we may or may not have cancer and the tests may or may not confirm this. This creates four possibilities. The hypothesis to be tested may be true or false and we may accept or reject it. In other words, we may accept a hypothesis that is true or false or reject a hypothesis that is true or false. The possibilities may be shown in diagram form:

Generic Template for Hypothesis Testing

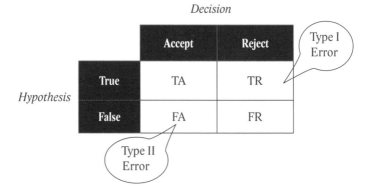

With respect to the previous chart: TA stands for "acceptance of a true hypothesis," TR stands for "rejection of a true hypothesis," FA stands for "acceptance of a false hypothesis," and FR stands for "rejection of a false hypothesis." Naturally, we wish to avoid the rejection of a true hypothesis, known as a Type I error, as well as avoid the acceptance of a false hypothesis, known as a Type II error.

Hypothesis testing will always involve the possibility of Type I and Type II errors. The risk of one of these errors will always be deemed greater than the other. Let's look at the hypothesis: "I do not have cancer." In this case, suppose the hypothesis is true and we reject it. We have committed a Type I error. Now suppose the hypothesis is incorrect and we accept it. Then we have committed a Type II error. Here, the Type II error is more serious than the Type I error. The Type II error would lead a person with cancer to go unchecked, with the cancer likely becoming more serious. The Type I error is not as serious, but would invariably prove detrimental. Not only would it be psychologically damaging to think that you did have cancer, but it could also be physically damaging if you were subjected to further tests and treatments.

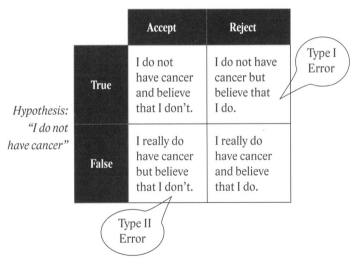

Decision

Hypothesis: "I do not have cancer"		Accept	Reject
	True	I do not have cancer and believe that I don't.	I do not have cancer but believe that I do. — Type I Error
	False	I really do have cancer but believe that I don't. — Type II Error	I really do have cancer and believe that I do.

Let's view another example in the context of the legal system: "The accused is not guilty." In this case, with reference to the following matrix, suppose the hypothesis is true and we reject it (thus committing a Type I error). A Type I error means that an innocent person has been found guilty. Now suppose the hypothesis is actually incorrect and we accept it (thus committing a Type II error). This means that a guilty person has been set free. In this situation, the Type I error is arguably more serious than the Type II error. After all, one need only recall the legal dictum: "Better that 10 guilty go free than one innocent be wrongfully convicted."

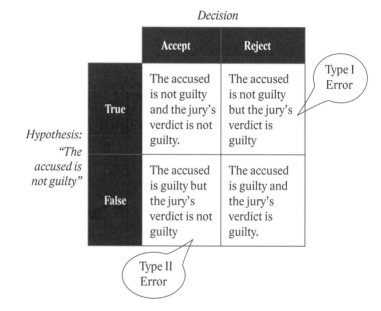

Decision

		Accept	Reject
Hypothesis: "The accused is not guilty"	**True**	The accused is not guilty and the jury's verdict is not guilty.	The accused is not guilty but the jury's verdict is guilty — Type I Error
	False	The accused is guilty but the jury's verdict is not guilty — Type II Error	The accused is guilty and the jury's verdict is guilty.

All research propositions should be analyzed in this manner. We should ask: "If the hypothesis is true, what are the consequences of rejection?... If the hypothesis is false, what are the consequences of acceptance?" Depending on our answer, we will risk committing one error more than the other.

In summary, it is unclear whether Type I or Type II errors are more serious. In the medical field, for instance, when dealing with disease and/or life and death situations, Type II errors are more serious. Within the legal system, especially for individuals on trial, Type I errors are arguably more serious. In the field of business, it is unclear which type of error is more detrimental. Whereas Type I errors may result in monetary loss and embarrassment, Type II errors represent lost opportunities. For more on how these two types of errors impact the field of commerce, see *Chapter 2*, page 43.

Note: It is worth mentioning the rationale behind why we state any hypothesis in the negative. In the previous two examples, we stated "I do not have cancer" and "The accused is not guilty" rather than "I do have cancer" and "The accused is guilty." In the world of science and statistics, hypotheses are always stated in the negative as we are trying to disprove a negative hypothesis rather than trying to prove a positive hypothesis. The rationale is that, scientifically speaking, we can never conclusively prove a positive hypothesis, but we can conclusively disprove a negative one. If we, as laypersons, find it more natural to employ a positive hypothesis, we should anticipate that Type I and Type II errors will reverse themselves. What we call a Type I error will become a Type II error and vice versa.

Per the discussion of Type I and Type II errors on page 43, the discussion assumes that the hypothesis was negatively stated: "The business deal (or movie deal) we are considering is not a great one." If we prefer a positive hypothesis, "The business deal (or movie deal) we are considering is a great one," we will find that the information regarding the Type I and Type II errors is reversed. Nonetheless, the conceptual nature of these two types of errors remains intact.

Prisoner's Dilemma

> **Tip #19:** The Prisoner's Dilemma provides an example of how cooperation is superior to competition.

Once upon a time, the police caught two suspects with ample counterfeit notes in their possession. The police knew the two men were acquaintances and escorted them to separate jail cells so they couldn't connive. The police knew the men were working in collusion but couldn't find the counterfeiting machine after a thorough search of each of their premises. Without solid evidence, the police knew the suspects would receive light sentences, as they had semi-plausible alibis.

Indeed, a confession was needed. The police decided to offer immunity to the first suspect who confessed and also offered up the location of the counterfeiting machine. This person would go free, and the other suspect would get a 10-year prison sentence. If they remained silent, they could each expect a three-year prison sentence for possession of multiple counterfeit bills. Each suspect was also told, out of judicial fairness, that if they both confessed they would each receive a seven-year prison sentence.

Each suspect faced four possible outcomes:

	My partner keeps quiet	My partner confesses
I keep quiet	We each get three years.	My partner goes free; I get ten years.
I confess	I go free; my partner gets ten years.	We each get seven years.

If you were one these suspects, what would you do?

First you might consider what your partner will do. Let's say that you both decide to keep quiet. If you keep quiet too, you get three years; if you confess, you go free. Thus, it's better for you to confess when your partner keeps quiet—you go free.

But what if he confesses? Now if you keep quiet, you get ten years; if you confess, you get seven years. Thus, if he confesses, it's also better for you to confess (results in three fewer years). Regardless of what he does, you avoid three years in jail by confessing.

It sounds like you should confess. The hitch—a big hitch—is that if he figures things out the same way, he's going to confess—just like you—and you will both get seven years, even though you both could have kept quiet and only received three years each.

This situation is called the Prisoner's Dilemma. The story was first told by economist A.W. Tucker in 1950. The police have probably known this game for a long time. So have criminals. It is just one version of a simple but compelling bargaining game.

The Prisoner's Dilemma is an example of a mixed-motive game: Both parties can do well if they work together by cooperating or they can try to gain an advantage over each other by competing. The fact that elements of both cooperation and competition are simultaneously present makes for mixed motives and contributes to the inherent complexity in these and similar games. After all, in the case of individuals, the "happiness" of one party depends not only on the choices he or she makes, but also is influenced by the choices made by the other party.

The Prisoner's Dilemma game is also an example of an individual versus group game. Here, we can choose to work for the group or for ourselves. When everyone in a group contributes (i.e., acts cooperatively), everyone benefits. If some people act individually, however, they keep what they might have contributed to the group, and they also share in what everyone else has contributed. It is the classic distinction between givers and takers. It is the basis for the conclusion that "nice people finish last."

Dilemmas that fit the requirements for a Prisoner's Dilemma often can be summarized as follows. The first word in each pair denotes the outcome of the first person; the second word in each pair denotes the outcome of the second person:

	My partner cooperates (He or she keeps quiet)	My partner does not cooperate (He or she confesses)
I cooperate (I keep quiet)	Win, Win (3 years, 3 years)	Lose, Win (10 years, 0 years)
I do not cooperate (I confess)	Win, Lose (0 years, 10 years)	Lose, Lose (7 years, 7 years)

If both parties cooperate, they are rewarded; if they both defect, they are punished. If one cooperates, but the other defects, the cooperator is the loser (or sucker or saint, depending on your point of view) and the non-cooperator is a winner (but traitor). In true Prisoner's Dilemma games, the winner's payoff always exceeds the loser's payoff (measured here in terms of fewer years served).

As highlighted, the aggregate benefit of cooperation exceeds the aggregate benefit of non-cooperation. For example, if both counterfeiters cooperate, they will serve an aggregate of 6 years of prison time (i.e., 3 + 3 = 6 years). If both counterfeiters fail to cooperate, they will serve a total of 14 years of prison time (i.e., 7 + 7 = 14 years). A middle ground arises when one person cooperates and the other doesn't because this leads to an aggregate of 10 years of prison time (either 10 + 0 = 10 years or 0 + 10 = 10 years).

Not surprisingly, expectations play a big role in how people respond to these dilemmas. In other human endeavors, if one person defects when the other cooperates, the pair faces a major crossroads. If one of two business partners, for instance, doesn't contribute as much as the other thought he or she would, they may have to work out a whole new arrangement. If two people pursue individual and mutually contradictory goals within a single partnership, the likelihood of "divorce" is imminent. When two people both contribute substantially to a growing relationship, "romance" can flourish.

Chapter 4

Analyzing Arguments

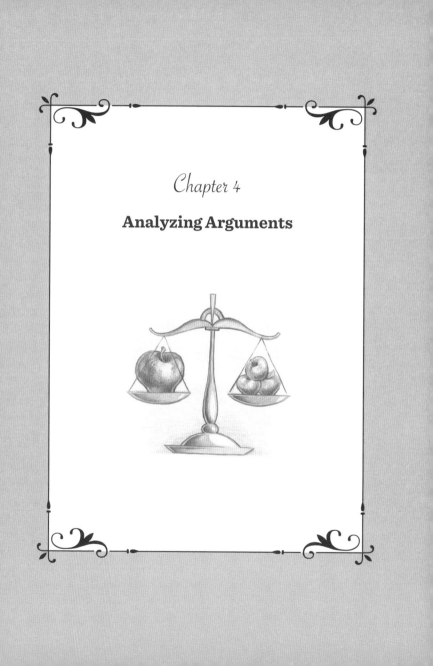

I can stand brute force, but brute reason is quite unbearable. There is something unfair about its use. It is hitting below the intellect.

—OSCAR WILDE

Overview

ARGUMENTS

What is an argument? An argument is not a heated exchange like the ones you might have had with a good friend, family member, or significant other. An argument, as referred to in logic, is "a claim or statement made which is supported by some evidence." A claim is part of a larger concept called "argument."

"Oh, it sure is a nice day today." This statement is certainly a claim, but it is not an argument because it contains no support for what is said. To turn it into an argument we could say, "Oh, it sure is a nice day today. We have had nearly five hours of sunshine." Now the claim ("it sure is a nice day") is supported by some evidence ("nearly five hours of sunshine").

Let's get some definitions out of the way.

DEFINITIONS

Conclusion: The conclusion is the claim or main point that the author, writer, or speaker is making.

Evidence: The evidence includes any facts, examples, statistics, surveys, and other information or data that the author (writer or speaker) uses in support of his or her conclusion.

Assumption: The assumption is the author's unstated belief ("unstated evidence") about why his or her claim is right. An assumption is that part of the argument that the author, writer, or speaker assumes to be correct without stating so; it is "that which the author takes for granted." More poetically, the assumption may be said to be "the glue that holds the evidence to the conclusion."

The ABCs of Argument Structure

Tip #20: Evidence + Assumption = Conclusion. The assumption is the glue that holds the evidence to the conclusion.

The following expresses the relationship between the three elements of classic argument structure:

Conclusion = Evidence + Assumption
or
Conclusion − Evidence = Assumption

The ability to understand simple but formal argument structure is useful, if not essential, to advance critical thinking. After identifying the conclusion and evidence, we then proceed to examine the third element, called the assumption. So how do we go about identifying the first two elements, the conclusion and evidence?

IDENTIFYING THE CONCLUSION AND EVIDENCE

Confusion may arise as to what part of an argument is evidence and what part is the conclusion. Certain "guide words" always signal the use of evidence or the start of the conclusion. The chart on the next page lists the most common guide words. If, for example, you hear someone say, "Because the economy is getting better, I'm going to buy a car," you may presume that the phrase "because the economy is getting better" is evidence. The reason for this is that the word "because" always signals the use of evidence. The remaining phrase "I'm going to buy a car" contains the conclusion. Note that these phrases may also be reversed without affecting what is the evidence and conclusion. For example, "I'm going to buy a car because the economy is getting better."

If possible, use guide words to identify the conclusion and evidence in an argument.

Words that always signal "evidence"	Words that always signal "conclusion"
• As	• As a result
• As indicated by	• Clearly
• As shown by	• Consequently
• Because	• Hence
• For	• In conclusion
• Given that	• So
• Since	• Therefore
• The reason is that	• Thus

It is important to note that guide words will not always be present to guide you, meaning that you cannot always rely on them to locate the conclusion and the evidence in an argument.

LOCATING THE ASSUMPTION

Whereas the conclusion and evidence in an argument are always explicit, the assumption is always implicit. The fact that assumptions are, by definition, implicit means that they will not be stated, that is, written down on paper or spoken out loud by the speaker. They exist foremost in the mind of the author or speaker. Conclusions and evidence, on the other hand, are explicit. This means that they will be stated—physically written down on paper or spoken out loud.

Evaluating Arguments

> **Tip #21:** There are effectively two ways to attack an argument: attack the evidence or attack the assumption(s).

In seeking to evaluate arguments, we must aggressively analyze each component. How strong is the evidence? How strong is the key assumption? Obviously, in order to attack the evidence and the assumption, we must be able to identify them.

Parts of an Argument	Stated or Implied	This means
Conclusion	Explicit	It is stated, i.e., written down or spoken out loud.
Evidence	Explicit	It is stated, i.e., written down or spoken out loud.
Assumption	Implicit	It is not stated (written down or spoken out loud), but remains in the mind of the person presenting the argument.

Short exercises: To practice using classic argument structure to evaluate arguments, fill in the missing pieces below—conclusion, evidence, and assumption. Proposed solutions start on the next page.

1. DOROTHY AND HER COLLEGE ENTRANCE EXAM

Argument: Since Dorothy achieved a high score on her college entrance exam, she will surely succeed in college.

Conclusion:

Evidence:

Assumption:

2. FINLAND

Argument: Finland is the most technologically advanced country in the world. More people per capita own mobile phones in Finland than anywhere else on earth.

Conclusion:

Evidence:

Assumption:

3. Taking on the World with a Smile

Argument: Dear Anita: You know, I get such a great feeling when I talk to my old high school friends and find out they're doing well. Just yesterday, I spoke with two of my high school buddies, Paul and Maxine, and have been in a good mood ever since. Say, I hear you're kind of down in the dumps lately. If you go home and call your high school friends, it will cheer you up and you will be ready to take on the world with a smile. Talk to you soon, Bill.

Conclusion:

Evidence:

Assumption:

4. Quick-Stop vs. Big-Buy Grocery Stores

Argument: I shop at Big-Buy grocery stores because prices are 10% less than at Quick-Stop grocery stores.

Conclusion:

Evidence:

Assumption:

1. Dorothy and her College Entrance Exam (Solution)

Argument: Since Dorothy achieved a high score on her college entrance exam, she will surely succeed in college.

Conclusion: Dorothy will surely succeed in college.

Evidence: She achieved a high score on her college entrance exam.

Assumption: Success on a college entrance exam leads to success in college or, stated another way, success in college requires the same set of skills as is required to perform well on a college entrance exam.

Let's evaluate the argument:

Attack the evidence

Did Dorothy really score high on her college entrance exam? How high is high? In other words, we need to find out what score she actually got and then verify that it was indeed a "high" score.

Attack the assumption

This argument assumes that a high test score is not only enough to get accepted to college in the first place, but also that it's a good predictor of success in college. First, the college admissions process also considers other factors, including a candidate's written application essays, extracurricular activities, personal/academic references, and even an interview. Second, other factors that are likely required for success in college are not related to taking a test. Succeeding on a test requires no interaction with anyone except oneself. What about other factors, such as personal motivation, independence, or emotional stability? Some courses may require group projects. In short, Dorothy may not have the personal qualities to succeed in college, even though she's mighty fine at taking an entrance exam!

2. *Finland (Solution)*

Argument: Finland is the most technologically advanced country in the world. More people per capita own mobile phones in Finland than anywhere else on earth.

Conclusion: Finland is the most technologically advanced country in the world.

Evidence: More people per capita own mobile phones in Finland than anywhere else on earth.

Assumption: Ownership of mobile phones is the best criterion for determining whether a country or its people are technologically advanced.

Let's evaluate this argument:

Attack the evidence

Even though people own phones, do they actually use them? Do they know how to use the vast majority of all the phone functions? Also, are mobile phones as technologically sophisticated in Finland as they are in other countries?

Attack the assumption

Perhaps ownership of mobile phones (per capita) is not the best criterion for determining technological advancement. Perhaps a better, more accurate criterion is ownership of computers or the ability to use computer software. Or perhaps the best criterion for determining technological advancement is the ability to manufacture technologically advanced equipment.

3. Taking on the World with a Smile (Solution)

Argument: Dear Anita: You know, I get such a great feeling when I talk to my old high school friends and find out they're doing well. Just yesterday, I spoke with two of my high school buddies, Paul and Maxine, and have been in a good mood ever since. Say, I hear you're kind of down in the dumps lately. If you go home and call your high school friends, it will cheer you up and you will be ready to take on the world with a smile. Talk to you soon, Bill.

Conclusion: If you go home and call your high school friends, it will cheer you up and you will be ready to take on the world with a smile.

Evidence: You know, I get such a great feeling when I talk to my old high school friends and find out they're doing well. Just yesterday, I spoke with Paul and Maxine and have been in a good mood ever since. Say, I hear you're kind of down in the dumps lately.

Assumption: In the same way that calling his high school friends "works" for Bill, it will also "work" for Anita.

Again, there are two ways to attack this argument:

Attack the evidence

Is Anita really feeling down? Are Bill's buddies actually doing well? Are Paul and Maxine actually the high school classmates of Bill?

Attack the assumption
Does Anita have high school friends? Are they also doing well? Upon hearing that Anita's high school friends are doing well, will she react as favorably as Bill did (hopefully Anita's not the jealous type)?

4. Quick-Stop vs. Big-Buy Grocery Stores (Solution)

Argument: I shop at Big-Buy grocery stores because prices are 10 percent less than at Quick-Stop grocery stores.

Conclusion: I shop at Big-Buy grocery stores.

Evidence: Prices are 10 percent less.

Assumption: Price is the decisive factor in determining where I shop for groceries. Or stated more simply, when choosing between Big-Buy and Quick-Stop, I choose based on price.

Let's attack the argument:

Attack the evidence
Are prices really 10 percent less at Big-Buy grocery stores? Are prices even cheaper at all? We need proof. Perhaps it's time to check grocery receipts to verify claims of lower prices. Don't just take for granted that all evidence is really "good" evidence. Moreover, is quality constant? If the quality between two items differs, better quality might warrant paying a higher price.

Attack the assumption
For example, we may want to attack the assumption by saying that price should not be the motivating factor as to where we shop. Perhaps location or proximity is a better criterion, or perhaps customer service should be the key factor influencing where we shop; perhaps store appearance and cleanliness should be the determining factor; perhaps prestige is the driving factor.

The Five Common Reasoning Flaws

Tip #22: The five most common critical reasoning errors that people make include: comparing "apples with oranges," over-generalizing on the basis of small samples, ignoring relevant evidence, confusing cause and effect, and failing to anticipate bottlenecks when plans are put into action.

When we speak of critical reasoning errors, we are referring largely to errors relating to the assumptions we make. Of the five common types of assumptions, the first category falls under comparison and analogy assumptions and requires that we compare two things which, although different, are logically equivalent. In general, we want to compare apples with apples and oranges with oranges, without mixing the two. The second category falls under representativeness assumptions. This reasoning error involves overgeneralizing on the basis of small samples or limited experience. In making the assumption that a sample is representative of the larger whole, we strengthen an argument. In making the assumption that the sample is not representative of the larger whole, the overall argument is weakened. The third category falls under "good evidence" assumptions. This reasoning error occurs when we take for granted that the evidence chosen is valid. The assumption that evidence chosen is objective, relevant, accurate, or truthful serves to strengthen any argument; the idea that evidence chosen is subjective, atypical, or spurious serves to weaken any argument. The fourth category falls within the topic of cause-and-effect assumptions. This reasoning error occurs if we mistakenly match cause with effect, or assume, without adequate evidence, that one event is the cause of another. The fifth category falls under implementation assumptions. This reasoning error arises from not anticipating bottlenecks when plans are put into action, and occurs whenever we assume outright that plans can be turned into action without significant impediments.

COMPARISON AND ANALOGY ASSUMPTIONS

We make comparisons based on people, places, things, or situations. Often it is done through analogy. What is an analogy? An analogy is a comparison of two (or more) items made on the basis that because they share one or more similarities, we can therefore assume they are alike in one or more other respects. An analogy is created every time a researcher delves into the realm of biological experimentation and compares the results done on animals, usually mice, to human beings. Sometimes, the comparison involves personal characteristics. We may see certain traits or characteristics in a father and son or mother and daughter and believe it is the basis for their sharing other similar characteristics. Other times, the comparison involves comparing two situations or events over different time periods. Many corporate decisions are still based on the idea that what has worked in the past will work in the future. International law is also, in large part, based on the principle of historical precedent.

The general strategy for attack is as follows:

Situation	Formulaically	How to attack the comparison
Are two things the same or nearly the same?	Does A = B?	Show that A is different from B and the comparison or analogy is weakened.
Are two things different?	Does A ≠ B?	Show that A is similar to B and the comparison or analogy is weakened.

In terms of evaluating or attacking comparisons, when two things are deemed similar, our goal will be to find dissimilarities in order to show that the two things are not alike. Consider the following example: "Martha did such a great job selling cutlery that we're going to promote her and put her in charge of condominium sales." What is being assumed is that sales ability is the key ingredient in making sales, and the type of product being sold is of secondary concern. How could we attack this argument? One way is to indicate that there could be a big difference between selling cutlery, a commodity product, and selling a condominium, a luxury good. A person effective at selling one type of product may be ineffective when selling another type. In the entrepreneurial context, a person successful in one industry may not be successful when switching to another industry.

In terms of evaluating or attacking comparisons, when two things are deemed dissimilar, our goal will be to find similarities in order to show that the two things are alike. For example, two male sports enthusiasts are having a beer, when one says to the other: "There is no comparison between athletes today and athletes of yesteryear. Mark Spitz won seven gold medals in swimming in the 1967 Mexico City Olympics, but his winning times are not good enough today to qualify for any of the men's Olympic swim events." To damage this argument, the second sports enthusiast might want to choose an example to show how athletes today are in some ways comparable to the athletes of yesteryear. For example, Jack Nicklaus' final round score of 271 in 1965 to win the Master's Golf Tournament in Augusta, Georgia, could be compared to Tiger Woods's final round score of 272 in 2002 to win the Master's Golf tournament on the exact same course. In this respect, by comparing two athletes in this manner, things do not look so dissimilar after all.

When comparing two things, particularly those across different time frames, we must be careful not to assume that information gathering techniques and, therefore, the quality of the data obtained are comparable. For example, any report comparing the findings of worker satisfaction levels in the 1940s to worker satisfaction levels today would be suspect, for no other reason than the difficulty of comparing the results of information gained under differing circumstances.

At the most fundamental level, we must ensure that the meaning and scope of words and terms used in an argument are consistently applied. Say, for example, we read that pollution is now ten times as bad in the suburban areas of our city as it was twenty years ago. Pollution may indeed by worse, but not by tenfold. What if the definition of pollution has changed to include air, water, noise, and garbage? This would certainly torpedo any attempt to establish a valid comparison.

REPRESENTATIVENESS ASSUMPTIONS

A sample is a group of people or things selected from a larger number of people or things that is presumably representative of the larger group or, as it is often said, "the population as a whole." We have all heard such statements as: "I've never met a person from country Z whom I liked" or "I highly recommend ABC Restaurant because the three times that I have dined there, the food has been delicious."

These two examples show representative sample assumptions in action. The first person obviously has not met all the people from country Z, and the second person obviously has not tried every dish in ABC Restaurant. For a sample to be representative, it must be both quantitatively and qualitatively representative. For a sample to be quantitatively sound, a large enough sample must be chosen. Obviously, the selection of one or two items is not enough. For a sample to be qualitatively sound, a random or diverse enough cross-sample of its members must be chosen.

What about a travel agency that claims "Three out of every four tourists recommend Morocco as a tourist destination." For all we know, only eight tourists were surveyed, and six of these recommend Morocco as a tourist destination. In this hypothetical case, the sample of tourists chosen was too small. Now let's assume that the statistic "three out of every four tourists recommend Morocco" was based on a sufficiently large sample of several hundred tourists. But what if all the tourists were from Africa? Or suppose all the tourists were male or owned a travel agency specializing in trips to Africa? All of a sudden, we would have doubts as to whether these several hundred tourists were representative of tourists in general, and the statement that three of four tourists recommend Morocco would be suspect.

When evaluating situations involving representativeness, the objective is to show how a particular person, place, or thing is not representative of the larger "whole" and the argument is weakened or falls apart. On the other hand, show how a particular person, place, or thing is representative of the larger "whole" and the argument is strengthened.

Generally, the issue will not be whether a sample is large enough but whether it is diverse enough. If the sample is not drawn from relevant representative subclasses, the sample size is of little consequence. A noteworthy real-life example is the Gallup poll, as devised by George Gallup, and used notably for predicting winning candidates in national political races. In order to generalize about the opinions of the people in an entire country with respect to a given candidate or political issue, data must be gathered from subclasses based on age, education, gender, geography, professional status, race, and perhaps even religion. Other subclasses, such as body weight and hair color, would be irrelevant. Even though there may well be millions of people in a given country, the Gallup poll requires a sample size of only about 1,800 people to be statistically accurate.

Note that a representativeness assumption is different from an analogy assumption. An analogy assumption might be thought of as a side-by-side comparison of two things whereas a representativeness assumption might be thought of as a vertical comparison stating that a "smaller something" is just like the larger whole. An analogy assumes big "A" is equal to big "B," but a representativeness assumption assumes little "a" is equal to big "A."

"Good Evidence" Assumptions

Arguments should be based on evidence which itself is valid. It is only human nature to want to choose relevant evidence that supports our stance while ignoring relevant evidence which refutes it. If we want to continue smoking, for example, we may entertain only that evidence which suits our fancy, such as "smoking helps me relax, looks cool, and keeps my weight down." Evidence contrary to this viewpoint, such as "smoking is dangerous to my health" or "smoking is too expensive," is ignored. For the person who doesn't like riding motorcycles, evidence chosen might include the ideas that motorcycles are dangerous and noisy, grease and dirt may ruin your clothes, helmets are uncomfortable, only two people can ride at once, and it is hard to ride motorcycles in rainy or snowy weather. Such a list might exclude the fact that motorcycles are fun and enjoyable to ride, more maneuverable, easy to find parking spaces for, and relatively inexpensive to purchase and maintain.

One of the hallmarks of objective thinking is that we should invite all relevant evidence to bear on an issue or decision at hand. We should not ignore or slant evidence if what we seek is the "truth." The legal system followed by most countries throughout the world is modeled on the adversarial justice system. These systems of justice lend themselves to the slanting of information and evidence. Trial lawyers for the defense and prosecution present evidence in a way which maximizes the chances of them winning cases. It is important to note, however, that judges and juries must remain impartial if fairness is to be achieved.

CAUSE-AND-EFFECT ASSUMPTIONS

Does one event really cause another? Cause and effect is concerned with the relationship (or non-relationship) between two events. We call the first event the cause and the second event the effect. When we write this as a formula, we use A for the cause and B for the effect: $A \rightarrow B$.

As depicted in **Exhibit 4.1**, cause-and-effect relationships arise under six potential categories. These include the following:

Exhibit 4.1 Coincidence, Correlation, and Causation

No Cause and Effect	Cause and Effect
I. Mere coincidence	IV. Legitimate causation
II. Low correlation	V. Alternative causation
III. High correlation	VI. Reverse causation

The first question we ask when a cause-and-effect assumption is on the horizon is whether any relationship exists between two items. There may not be any plausible relationship. For example, "The street light turned red just before the cat fell out of the tree; therefore, the red light caused the cat to fall out of the tree" has no plausible causal relationship (mere coincidence). Next, assuming a relationship exists, we ask whether the two events are causally related or merely correlated. If a correlation exists, we seek to determine whether that correlation is low or high. If causally related, we seek to determine whether the two events are legitimately correlated or whether alternative or reverse causation is at work.

Here are further explanations of the categories highlighted in the previous chart.

I. Mere Coincidence
"Every time I sit in my favorite seat during a playoff game, our team wins." It is implausible that your "lucky" seat is causing your sports team to win. And it is equally implausible that a regular or "bad" seat will cause your team to lose.

II. Low Correlation
An example of low correlation might be the opening of new health clubs in your city and the general level of fitness among citizens in your

city. Obviously, the opening of health clubs with facilities that include weight-lifting classes, aerobic classes, and exercise machines will have some effect on the fitness level of people in general. But, practically, it will not have a great deal of impact. The direct impact of a small number of health club members on a city's larger population is limited. Even if there is a general trend toward more fitness in your city, it may be because people walk, ride bikes, or take hikes more often. Individuals may participate in these activities and not be associated with health clubs.

III. High Correlation (but not causation)

Certain factors or characteristics are strongly correlated—for example, being tall and being a National Basketball Association player. Not every player in the NBA is tall, but the vast majority of players are. We can safely say that there is a strong correlation between being tall and being an NBA player. A classic example in business is a company's sales and advertising costs. The more a company spends on advertising, the greater its sales. (The correlation between advertising and sales is approximately +0.8.) Other examples might include hot weather and ice cream sales, or rainy weather and umbrella sales. Strongly correlated events may be talked about as if they are causally related. It is important to be able to draw the line between high correlation and actual causation.

IV. Legitimate Causation

The law of gravity indicates a causal relationship. I throw an apple up into the air and it comes back down. Other events are so highly correlated that for all practical purposes they are assumed to be causally related—for example, the amount of coffee consumed and the amount of coffee beans consumed or the number of babies born and the number of baby diapers used. However, it would not be accurate to say that the number of coffee beans *grown* or the number of baby diapers *manufactured* are likewise causally related.

V. Alternative Explanation

Alternative explanation can be called alternative causal explanation. Here we agree on a single conclusion (the effect) but differ as to which is the correct cause. We must always be on guard for the existence of another cause whenever it looks as though two events are otherwise causally related. A business may have increased its advertising budget and seen an increase in sales. It is easy to view these two events as causally connected. But advertising may be having little or no effect on sales. The reason that sales have increased may be that a major competitor of the company went out of business. The following is a more involved example: "It's plain to see that the recent spike in high school shootings is the result of viewing violent TV programming." Who's to say that the high school shootings are not instead the result of more lax gun laws, dwindling educational standards, or weakened religious following? (In this case, it is not A that is causing B but rather C that is causing B.) Or maybe a third factor is causing both A and B. For example, perhaps both the increase in high school shootings and the increase in violent TV programming are the result of a third factor, e.g., breakdown of the family unit. (In this latter case, it is not A that is causing B but rather C that is causing both A and B.)

VI. Reverse Causation

Does your favorite commercial fiction author sell a lot of books because he or she is famous, or is he or she famous as a result of selling lots of books? Reverse causation is tricky. You think X is causing Y, but in reality it is Y that is causing X. The following example helps illustrate this point. Say you notice that a young woman at work named Sally is always working hard. And you say to yourself one day: "Sally is a hard worker. No wonder our boss gives her the toughest assignments." The argument becomes, "Because Sally is such a hard worker, our boss gives her the toughest assignments." But could the reverse be true? What if Sally is lazy and not naturally such a hard worker, but rather works hard only because she happens to be given the toughest projects?

Now the argument becomes: "Because Sally is given such tough work projects, she is therefore forced to work hard!" Children may reveal funny examples to illuminate the concept of reverse causation. Young children may believe that firemen cause fires, for every time they see a picture or a video of a fire, there are firemen at the scene. Eventually, the reverse is confirmed to be true: "Fires cause firemen."

As an historical example, when researchers first started testing the hypothesis that "smoking causes cancer," one of the first things they considered was the reverse hypothesis—the idea that people who have cancer might try smoking (i.e., cancer causes smoking). Not surprisingly, this hypothesis proved groundless. However, in many other situations it is difficult to distinguish between the cause and the effect. Consider the statement: "You're good at the things you like." The cause-and-effect argument becomes, "You like things (cause), and therefore you become good at them (effect)." But could it be that you find yourself good at some things and then learn to like them?

IMPLEMENTATION ASSUMPTIONS

Some years ago, an article in a Western travel magazine stated: "Because air travel is becoming so convenient and because people have greater disposable incomes, soon everyone will have been to Africa to see the lions."

Yet today, few people outside of Africa can claim to have been to Africa to see the lions. What accounts for the discrepancy between the travel magazine article and people actually going to visit Africa and the lions? Was the article wrong about plane travel becoming more convenient or people having higher levels of disposable income? The magazine was not likely wrong in these respects. However, the article was incorrect in its prediction that "everyone" (or, less literally, "many people") would go to Africa to see the lions. The discrepancy between an otherwise sound plan and action is based on the assumption that a sound plan must necessarily achieve its desired result. This is not necessarily so.

Why do plans not always work? There are essentially four major reasons that plans do not work: (1) an individual or organization's lack of desire, motivation, or perseverance; (2) an individual or organization's lack of prerequisite skill or technological capability to carry out the plan; (3) lack of required opportunity or wherewithal—economic resources—to commence or complete a given task; and (4) unanticipated bottlenecks or consequences (physical, financial, technological, or logistical) arising from the plan's implementation. "Implementation assumptions" are grounded on the idea that a plan will work because of an absence of the kinds of deficiencies cited above.

First, an individual or organization may lack desire, motivation, or perseverance to carry out a plan. There is a saying that "one who can read but doesn't is no better than one who cannot read." The ability to do something is not the same thing as actually using that skill. We all know of examples of extremely talented individuals who lack the focus or perseverance to achieve their true potential.

Second, the required skill or technological capability to carry out the plan may be lacking. Consider the statement a high school graduate made: "Either I'm going to medical school or I am going to join the military and become a member of the Special Forces." This assumes that the person has the talent and perseverance to get accepted to medical school en route to becoming a doctor. It equally assumes the physical and technical skill, mental toughness, and temperament to make it through training en route to being selected as a member of the Special Forces.

Third, we cannot assume that an individual or organization has the required opportunity or financial wherewithal, that is, economic resources, to complete a given task. In the example above, the high school graduate assumes that in the case of medical school, he or she has the ability to also obtain loans and other forms of financial aid required to complete medical studies.

Fourth, in terms of unanticipated bottlenecks or consequences, think what would happen if everyone pursued the proposed plan.

For example, your office may be considering the installation of a new computer software system, which many believe will resolve your company's communication problems. But if coworkers find the system too complicated and difficult to use, they may avoid using it (physical and technological limitations).

Be suspicious of any claim that suggests that legislation can solve a problem. Legislation can certainly be used to discourage or limit undesirable actions, but it does not prevent them per se. Legislation to prevent discrimination, for instance, may not work if people themselves are unwilling to stop discrimination. Likewise, passing a law to increase fines for people parking their cars illegally in front of prestigious shopping venues will not necessarily stop shoppers from parking their cars, particularly wealthy consumers who may nonetheless decide to park illegally and accept higher fines.

The following section provides an opportunity to solve critical reasoning problems. These multiple-choice problems are grouped according to the five categories introduced here: comparison and analogy assumptions, representativeness assumptions, "good evidence" assumptions, cause-and-effect assumptions, and implementation assumptions.

Testing Critical Reasoning

Tip #23: Watch for "scope shifts," which occur when one term is substituted for another as an argument unfolds.

PROBLEM 12   CRIME

According to an article in the Life and Times section of the Sunday newspaper, crime is on the downturn in our city. Police initiatives, neighborhood watches, stiff fines, and lengthened prison terms have all played a significant role in reducing the number of reported crimes by 20 percent.

Which of the following would most weaken the belief that crime has decreased in our city?

A) In its Sunday newspaper, a neighboring city has also reported a decrease in crime.

B) Police officers were among those citizens who voted for a bill to support police initiatives to reduce crime in our city.

C) Most of the recent police arrests were repeat offenders.

D) The author of the article includes white-collar crime in his definition of crime, thus increasing the number of reported crimes.

E) It is possible for reported crime to have gone down while actual crime has remained the same or actually gone up.

Tip #24: Changes in the way words are defined destroy the ability to make valid comparisons.

PROBLEM 13   HYPERACTIVITY

Viewing children as more hyperactive today than they were ten years ago, many adults place the blame squarely on the popularity of video games and multimedia entertainment.

What the following revelations would most undermine the argument above?

A) Even if children today are more hyperactive than they were ten years ago, they are widely viewed as more spontaneous and creative.

B) The claim that children are more aggressive today is a more serious charge than their being considered more hyperactive.

C) Children's books published in recent years contain on average more pictures than do children's books published in the past.

D) More types of behavior are deemed hyperactive today than were ten years ago.

E) Incidences of ailments such as Attention Deficit Hyperactivity Disorder (ADHD) are reported to be on the increase in recent years.

Tip #25: If a situation involves a "survey," check to see if the survey is based on a sample which is both quantitatively and qualitatively representative.

PROBLEM 14   MOVIE BUFFS

According to a recent survey, any sequel to the movie *Victim's Revenge* will not fare well. Respondents to a recent survey of moviegoers leaving Sunday matinees around the country indicated that movies based on serial killers with psychopathic tendencies have fallen out of vogue with current movie buffs. Therefore, if movie studios want to produce films that are financially successful, they should avoid producing such films.

Which of the following would most weaken the idea that film studios should stop production of stories and dramas based on serial killers with psychopathic tendencies?

A)   Movie stars have a significant following of people who see their every film.

B)   People who attend Sunday matinees are not representative of the views of the moviegoing population as a whole.

C)   The film *Psycho*, originally directed by Alfred Hitchcock, was a big hit in 1960 and was remade in 1998.

D)   Both student enrollment in college criminology courses and book sales based on the lives of real-life serial killers are up.

E)   The cost of making such movies requires skillful actors who can portray emotional conflict and intellectualism, and these actors demand high salaries.

Tip #26: Representativeness assumptions are based on the idea that some smaller "thing" is representative of the larger whole.

Problem 15   Bull Market

"Wow, the economy of India sure is strong. The National Stock Exchange (NSE) has gone up by more than 1,000 points since the beginning of the year."

Which of the following would lend the strongest support for the speaker's comments above?

A) The National Stock Exchange (NSE) is a fair indicator by which to judge the strength of the overall Indian economy.

B) The Bombay Stock Exchange (BSE) index has also gone up nearly 500 points since the beginning of the year.

C) The National Stock Exchange (NSE) index was actually down during this exact time last year.

D) During the same time period in which the Indian economy was considered strong, the economies of Asia and Europe were also considered strong.

E) The National Stock Exchange (NSE) Index, historically, is subject to great fluctuations.

Tip #27: Broadly speaking, representativeness assumptions occur any time that we argue from the particular to the general.

Problem 16   Putting

"Are you having trouble getting the golf score you deserve? Is putting your pariah? The new Sweet Spot Putter is designed to improve your golf game overnight without intensive lessons. Even rank amateurs can dramatically increase their putting accuracy by 25 percent. You too can achieve a low golf score with the new Sweet Spot Putter."

Someone who accepted the reasoning in the advertisement above would be making which one of the following assumptions?

A) Without quality equipment, a golf player cannot improve his or her game.

B) The new Sweet Spot Putter will improve an amateur's game more than it will improve a professional's game.

C) The quality of a person's golf game is largely determined by the accuracy of his or her putting.

D) The new Sweet Spot Putter is superior to any other putter currently on the market.

E) Lessons are not as effective at improving the accuracy of a player's putting as is the use of quality equipment.

Tip #28: Check to see whether evidence has been handpicked to support a claim being made. Otherwise we may fall victim to "proof by selected instances."

PROBLEM 17 CRITIC'S CHOICE

In a newly released book, *Decline of the Novelist*, the author argues that novelists today lack technical skills that were common among novelists during the past century. In this regard, the book might be right, since its analysis of 200 novels—100 contemporary and 100 non-contemporary—demonstrates convincingly that few contemporary novelists exhibit the same skill level as that of non-contemporary novelists.

Which of the following points to the most serious logical flaw in the critic's argument?

A) The title of the author's book could cause readers to accept the book's thesis even before they read the literary analysis of those novels that supports it.

B) There could be criteria other than the novelist's technical skills by which to evaluate a novel.

C) The novels the critic chose to analyze could be those that most support the book's thesis.

D) The particular methods novelists currently use may require even more literary skill than do methods used by writers of screenplays.

E) A reader who was not familiar with the language of literary criticism might not be convinced by the book's analysis of its 200 novels.

Tip #29: "Evidence omitted" may hold the key to determining an argument's validity.

PROBLEM 18   TEMPERAMENT

STEVE: Rick and Harriet, two of my red-haired friends, are irritable. It seems true that red-haired people have bad tempers.

JOHN: That's ridiculous. Red-haired people are actually quite docile. Jeff, Muriel, and Betsy—three of my red-haired friends—all have placid demeanors.

Which of the statements below provides the most likely explanation for the two seemingly contradictory statements above?

A) The number of red-haired people whom Steve knows may be different from the number of red-haired people whom John knows.

B) The number of red-haired people whom both Steve and John know may not be greater in total than the number of non-red-haired people whom both Steve and John know.

C) It is likely that Steve or John has incorrectly assessed the temperament of one or more of his red-haired friends.

D) It is likely that both Steve and John have friends who are not red-haired and yet also have bad tempers.

E) The examples that Steve uses and the examples that John uses to support their conclusions are likely both valid.

Tip #30: Correlation does not equal causation.

PROBLEM 19   CYCLIST

Touring professional cyclists have been shown to have between 4 and 11 percent body fat. If we could all decrease our body fat to that level, we could all cycle at a world-class level.

Which one of the following most accurately characterizes the method of reasoning used in the above statements?

A) Its conclusion is based on evidence, which in turn, is based on its conclusion.

B) It illustrates the absurdity of the argument by reaching an illogical conclusion.

C) It assumes a causal relationship between two highly correlated events.

D) It uses flawed evidence to support its conclusion.

E) It assumes what it seeks to establish.

Tip #31: Cause-and-effect assumptions are grounded in the idea that because one event follows another in time, the first of the two events is the cause and the second is the effect.

PROBLEM 20   SAT SCORES

Parents are too easily impressed with the recent rise in average SAT scores at the top American undergraduate universities and colleges. Unfortunately, this encouraging statistic is misleading. Scores have risen not because students possess better math, English, and writing skills but because students are better at taking tests. For those students accepted as undergraduates at the top universities and colleges, studies confirm that skills in the basics of reading, writing, and mathematics have been on the gradual decline over the past twenty years.

The author argues primarily by

A) Denying the accuracy of his opponents' figures

B) Finding an alternative explanation for his opponent's evidence

C) Introducing irrelevant information to draw attention away from the main issue

D) Employing circular reasoning

E) Suggesting that his opponent's evidence may be flawed

Tip #32: When tackling cause-and-effect scenarios, think first in terms of alternative causal explanations. If the argument states that A is causing B, then check to see that another cause, namely C, is not instead causing B.

PROBLEM 21 VALDEZ

Since Ana Valdez was installed as president of the Zipco Corporation, profits have averaged 15 percent each year. During her predecessor's tenure, the corporation's profits averaged only 8 percent per year. Obviously Ms. Valdez's aggressive international marketing efforts have caused the acceleration in the growth of Zipco's profits.

Which of the following, if true, would most weaken the conclusion drawn above?

A) During the tenure of Ms. Valdez's predecessor, the corporation began an advertising campaign aimed at capturing consumers in developing countries between the ages of nineteen and twenty-five.

B) The corporation's new manufacturing plant, constructed in the past year, has a 35 percent greater production capacity.

C) Since Ms. Valdez became president, the corporation has switched the primary focus of its advertising from print ads to radio and television commercials.

D) Ms. Valdez hired a well-known headhunting firm which found talented vice-presidents for two of the corporation's five divisions.

E) Just before Ms. Valdez took over as president, her predecessor, Mr. Jones, directed the acquisition of a rival corporation, which has nearly doubled the corporation's yearly revenues.

Tip #33: A more complex form of alternative explanation occurs when two effects result from a single cause. Thus, if an argument suggests that A is causing B, consider the possibility that another cause, namely C, could be causing both A and B.

Problem 22   Headline

The headline of the *College Tribune* reads: "Obesity Linked to Depression."

Which of the following, if true, would most weaken the implied conclusion drawn between becoming overweight and falling into depression?

A) An obese person may not understand why he or she is depressed or how to escape from the throes of depression.

B) Depression can also result from things other than obesity.

C) Low self-esteem is frequently cited as the cause of both obesity and depression.

D) A person twice as overweight as another person is not likely to be twice as depressed.

E) Depression has in turn been linked to desperation and suicide.

Tip #34: If A is thought to be causing B, the idea that B is causing A is called reverse causation and casts serious doubt on the notion that A is really causing B.

Problem 23   TV Viewing

An investigator divided 128 adults into two distinct groups (high TV viewers and low TV viewers) based on the number of hours of violent TV programming they watched per day. A significantly larger percentage of the high-viewing group than of the low-viewing group demonstrated a high level of aggression. The investigator concluded that greater TV viewing, particularly of violent programming, caused higher aggression levels.

Which of the following, if true, most seriously weakens the conclusion above?

A) Some subjects in the high-viewing group experienced lower levels of aggression than did other subjects in the high-viewing group.

B) Some subjects in the low-viewing group did not experience any aggression.

C) Fear of aggressive tendencies as a result of watching large amounts of TV was the reason some subjects restricted their viewing of TV.

D) Some subjects watched live programming whereas other viewers watched pre-recorded TV programs.

E) Some subjects' already-high levels of aggression caused them to increase their viewing, particularly of violent TV programs.

Tip #35: Test the opposite scenario—if you hear that a full moon causes the crime rate to rise, always ask what the crime rate is like when the moon is not full.

PROBLEM 24 SHARK

In a marine reserve off the south coast of Australia, people sometimes are attacked by sharks. Here, it is believed that the sharks will only attack people who are mistaken for seals, which occurs when surfers wear entirely black body suits. So for the past few years, surfers have started wearing bright metallic body suits. While many area residents remain skeptical, no surfer wearing a metallic body suit has yet been attacked by a shark.

Which of the statements below, if true, would best support the argument of those who advocate the use of metallic body suits?

A) Surfers at other surf areas who wear metallic body suits have not been attacked recently by sharks.

B) A number of surfers in this marine area wearing black body suits have been attacked recently by sharks.

C) No sharks have been spotted in this marine reserve off the south coast of Australia in recent months.

D) Some of the surfers who wear metallic suits also wear wristbands that contain metal bells in order to frighten away any sharks.

E) Underwater divers have observed sharks attacking tuna and other ocean fish, some of them black in color.

Tip #36: Theory may be divorced from practice. Plans may not equal completed action. Do not assume that plans will be implemented without a hitch.

PROBLEM 25   SOLAR ENERGY

Energy from the sun suffers none of the major problems of more traditional energy sources, such as oil, coal, and nuclear energy. It requires no imports from foreign countries, it creates no air and water pollution, it threatens no one with death from radiation, and it cannot be withheld by powerful utility monopolies. Therefore, we should encourage families to use solar energy.

Which of the following statements, if true, most seriously weakens the argument in the passage above?

A) There have been very few studies on the use of solar energy in the average household.

B) Most of the studies critical of solar energy have been conducted by powerful utility monopolies.

C) Research has not yet developed an effective way to capture and store solar energy in a way that most individual families can employ.

D) Federal price controls on domestically produced crude oil and natural gas could reduce the cost of fuel to the average family.

E) The cost of building and installing the apparatus needed to collect enough solar energy for a family of four is equal to the amount a family of four would pay for oil, coal, or nuclear-based energy in one year.

Tip #37: "Can" does not equal "will." The ability to do something should not imply application of that ability, whether due to choice or neglect.

PROBLEM 26   CLASSICS

Any literate person who is not lazy can read the classics. Since few literate persons have read the classics, it is clear that most literate persons are lazy.

Which of the following is an assumption on which the argument above is based?

A) Only literate persons can understand the classics.
B) Any literate person should read the classics.
C) Any literate person who is lazy has no chance of reading the classics.
D) Any literate person who will not read the classics is lazy.
E) Any literate person who can read the classics will choose to do so.

Tip #38: One way to uncover implementation assumptions is to anticipate bottlenecks.

PROBLEM 27   PUBLIC TRANSPORTATION

People should switch from driving their cars to work on weekdays to taking public transportation, such as buses and subways. In major cities such as New York, London, or Tokyo, for example, cars are an expensive and inefficient means of transportation, and fossil fuel emissions are the major source of the city's pollution.

The argument above makes all of the following assumptions EXCEPT

A) There may be easier ways to combat pollution in large cities than by having people switch to taking public transportation.

B) There are enough people who actually own cars, which are currently being used to drive to work, to make this plan realistically feasible.

C) Public transportation is both available and accessible should someone wish to switch.

D) Current public transportation systems can accommodate all the people who decide to switch.

E) The city can afford to pay public transport drivers and related personnel who may otherwise remain idle once the morning and evening rush hour periods are over.

Tip #39: An argument may depend on the assumption that a person or organization is aware of a pre-existing fact, situation, or condition.

PROBLEM 28   RAINBOW CORPORATION

"Tina obviously cares little about the environment. She continues to use Purple Rider Felt Pens even though the company that makes these pens, Rainbow Corp., has been the focus of several recent newspaper articles as a result of its indictment for several violations involving dumping toxic wastes in the harbor."

Which of the following would most weaken the claim that Tina cares little about the environment?

A) Although the Rainbow Corp. has been the subject of several newspaper articles, it has been praised by consumers for its high-quality products.

B) Tina is not aware of the recent newspaper articles which feature Rainbow Corp. and its indictment for several violations involving dumping toxic wastes in the harbor.

C) The newspaper which ran the articles of Rainbow's indictments also owns a "gossip magazine" called the *Tipsy Tattler*.

D) The public relations department of Rainbow Corp. never issued a statement denying that the company violated the law.

E) Tina was a member of an environmental protection organization during her freshman and sophomore years in college.

Tip #40: Searching for something does not guarantee that we'll recognize it once we've found it. The ability to accurately identify that which we are seeking to find may be a key assumption.

Problem 29   Personality

The interview is becoming an integral part of the admissions process at most graduate business programs. Since personality is deemed important to success not only in business school but also on the job, feedback from interviews will help the admissions office select candidates whose personalities are suited for business school and the workplace.

Which of the following is a fundamental assumption in the argument above?

A) Admission efforts will be successful if they include interviews.

B) The interview is becoming the most important element in the business school admissions process.

C) Interviewers can accurately identify those applicants whose personalities are suited and unsuited to success in business school.

D) The sole purpose of the interview from the eyes of the admissions office is to evaluate whether business school applicants' personalities are suited to the business school environment.

E) Interviews will be held at similar times of the day and will be conducted in venues that are reasonably comparable.

Putting It All Together

Tip #41: Always look for potentially vague terms in an argument and ask for or seek clarification.

PROBLEM 30   YUPPIE CAFÉ

For the purposes of reinforcing techniques used to analyze arguments, write or outline a response to the following argument.

The following appeared as part of a campaign to get local businesses to advertise on the Internet and through social media.

"The Yuppie Café began advertising on the Internet this year and was delighted to see its business increase by 15 percent over last year's total. Their success shows that you too can use the Internet to make your business more profitable."

Analyze the above argument according to classic argument structure, identifying the conclusion, evidence, and at least three assumptions. How persuasive do you find this argument? What would make this argument more persuasive?

Chapter 5

Mastering Logic

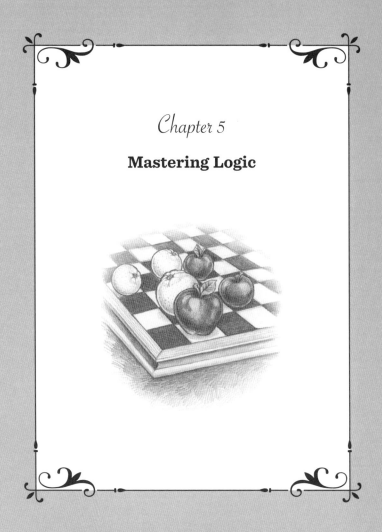

When you have eliminated the impossible,
whatever remains, however improbable,
must be the truth.

—SHERLOCK HOLMES

Overview

This chapter focuses on four interrelated topics:

1. "If...then" statements
2. "No-some-most-all" statements
3. Mutual inclusivity and exclusivity
4. Logical equivalency statements

To introduce formal logic, consider the following statements:

Original: If you work hard, you'll be successful.

Now ponder these related statements.

Statement 1: If you're successful, then you've worked hard.
Statement 2: If you don't work hard, you won't be successful.
Statement 3: If you're not successful, then you didn't work hard.

The question becomes: Which of the above statements are logical deductions based on the original statement above?

Upon closer examination, statement 1 isn't necessarily correct. The fact that you're successful (whatever this means!) doesn't mean that you have necessarily worked hard. There could be several other ways to become successful. For example, perhaps you're skillful, intelligent, or downright lucky.

Likewise, statement 2 is not necessarily correct. Just because you don't work hard doesn't mean that you won't be successful. As already mentioned, you might be skillful, intelligent, or lucky as opposed to hardworking. However, statement 3 is a perfectly logical deduction based on the original. If you're not successful, then you must not have worked hard. This doesn't mean, however, that there are not other explanations for why you might not have been successful. For example, perhaps you were neither intelligent in your approach nor skillful or lucky in your application.

"If . . . Then" Statements

"If . . . then" statements are another way to represent causal relationships. Take the following generic statement: "If A, then B." This is sometimes written in a more formulaic manner: i.e., "If A → B." Consider the statement "If it is U.S. money (dollar bills), then it is green (colored)." This can also be written: If $US → Green. Another way to illustrate an "if . . . then" relationship is to draw circles. The "If" item always represents the innermost circle while the "then" item always represents the outermost circle. See **Exhibit 5.1**.

Exhibit 5.1   Diagramming "If . . . then" Statements
If it is U.S. money, then it is green (if US$, then Green)

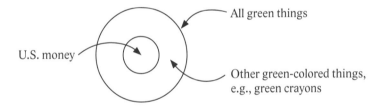

The above diagram illustrates in picture form the relationship between U.S. money and all green things. We can read from the inside circle to the outside circle, but we cannot read from the outside circle to the inside circle. "If U.S. money then green" does not equal "If green then U.S. money."

What can we logically infer from this type of statement? **Exhibit 5.2** contains four statements that may seem to the casual observer all to be inferable. However, only the fourth version is correctly inferable. In "if . . . then" statements, it is important that you read in one direction only, as the reverse is not necessarily true. Based on the original statement "If it is U.S. money, then it is green," the only thing we can infer logically from this statement is that it is true that "If it is not green, then it is not U.S. money."

Exhibit 5.2   American Money

Statement	Are these statements logically inferable?
(1) If it is U.S. money, then it is green.	n/a—original statement
(2) If it is green, then it is U.S. money.	No. This statement now says that all green things are U.S. money, and this is obviously ridiculous. Many things in the universe are green, including green-colored crayons, Christmas trees, garbage pails, green paint, and Kermit the Frog. (Known as the fallacy of affirming the consequent.)
(3) If it is not U.S. money, then it is not green.	No. Why? Many things other than U.S. money are green in color. (Known as the fallacy of denying the antecedent.)
(4) If it is not green, then it is not U.S. money.	Yes. This statement is inferable. Why? Because being green is one of the requirements for something to be U.S. money.

To master "if . . . then" statements it is essential to memorize the information contained in **Exhibit 5.3**. According to formal logic, the contrapositive is always correct. That is to say, the only thing we can infer from an "If A, then B statement" is the following: "If not B, then not A."

Exhibit 5.3   The Logic of "If ... then" Statements

Statement	Reference to formal logic	Are the statements logically inferable?
(1) If A, then B	n/a – (original statement)	n/a – (original statement)
(2) If B, then A	Known as the fallacy of affirming the consequent.	No, incorrect. This is not inferable.
(3) If not A, then not B	Known as the fallacy of denying the antecedent.	No, incorrect. This is not inferable.
(4) If not B, then not A	Known as the contrapositive.	Yes, correct. This is always logically inferable based on the original statement.

Another way of understanding "If ... then" statements is through an understanding of necessary versus sufficient conditions. A necessary condition must be present for an event to occur but will not, by itself, cause the given event to occur. A sufficient condition is enough, by itself, to ensure that the event will occur. In more technical parlance, a necessary condition is a condition which, if absent, will not allow the event to occur. A sufficient condition is a condition which, if present, will cause the event to occur.

When a person argues "If A, then B" and then argues "If B, then A," he or she erroneously reverses the conditional statement. The reason that a conditional statement cannot be reversed is that the original "If ... then" statement functions as a necessary condition. When it is reversed, an "If ... then" statement erroneously turns into a sufficient condition. Per **Exhibit 5.2**, being "green" is a necessary but not a sufficient condition in order for something to be considered U.S. money. Obviously, other factors besides "green coloring" need be present, including special watermarked paper, unique insignia, and precise size. By reversing the "If . . . then" statement, we erroneously suggest that being green-colored is enough of a criterion for something to be considered U.S. money.

Try one more example: "I gave my pet hamster water every day and he still died." Giving your pet hamster water each day is a necessary condition for keeping him alive, but it is not a sufficient condition. Obviously, a hamster needs many other things besides water, one of which is food.

"No-Some-Most-All" Statements

Many errors are committed in drawing inferences because ordinary speech is inherently ambiguous. For example, take the four statements below:

    I. No As are Bs
    II. All As are Bs
    III. Some As are Bs
    IV. Most As are Bs

To study the meaning of these four statements, refer to **Exhibit 5.4.** We can see that statement I corresponds to either diagram (1a) or (1b), but usually to diagram (1a). Statement II could represent either diagram (2a) or (2b), although usually diagram (2b). Statement III could typify any one of diagrams (3a), (3b), or (3c), although usually (3b). Statement IV could refer to either diagram (4a) or (4b), but typically (4b). This is evidence that ordinary speech can hamper clear thinking, and that it is often necessary to use non-verbal symbols to reinforce clear thinking.

There are two major differences between "most" and "some" statements. First, it is assumed that "most" implies majority (greater than half), while "some" implies minority (less than half). Second, whereas "some statements" automatically imply reciprocality, "most statements" do not necessarily imply reciprocality. For example, the statement "some doctors are wealthy people" implies that some wealthy people are also doctors. But the statement "most doctors are wealthy people" does not necessarily mean that most wealthy people are doctors.

The diagrams in **Exhibit 5.4** summarize the concepts of mutual inclusivity, mutual exclusivity, and overlap. Either circles are embedded inside one another, or circles are completely separated, or circles overlap with one another. Basically, there are nine possibilities.

Exhibit 5.5 provides a summary of logical equivalency statements. With a better understanding of the visual representations of these relationships, the next step is to be able to combine these visuals with verbal logic statements expressed in English. This is a translation exercise. For example, within the first column ("mutual inclusivity"), we must be able to see that all of the following are equivalent forms: "All cats are mammals"; "Every cat is a mammal"; "If it is a cat, then it is a mammal"; "Only mammals are cats"; and "No cat is not a mammal."

Mutual Inclusivity and Exclusivity

Exhibit 5.4   Overlap and Non-Overlap Scenarios
Statement I—*No As are Bs*—refers to either diagram (1a) or (1b).

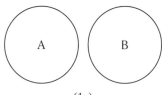
(1a)
A and B do not overlap
and are not touching.

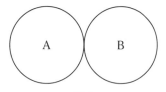
(1b)
A and B do not overlap
but are touching.

Exhibit 5.4 (*Cont'd*)

Statement II—*All As are Bs*—could refer to either diagram (2a) or (2b).

(2a)
A and B overlap perfectly.

(2b)
A is included in and
completely inside B.

Statement III—*Some As are Bs*—could refer to any of diagrams (3a), (3b), or (3c).

(3a)
B is included in and
completely inside A.

(3b)
A and B overlap
but only partly so.

(3c)
A and B overlap.
Most of B is inside
A but most of A is
not inside B.

Statement IV—*Most As are Bs*—could refer to either diagram (4a) or (4b).

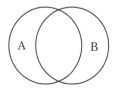

(4a)
A and B overlap. Most of A
is inside B and most of B is
inside A.

(4b)
A and B overlap. Most of A
is inside B, but most of B is
not inside A.

Statements of Logical Equivalency

Exhibit 5.5   Logical Equivalency Statements

	Mutual inclusivity	Mutual exclusivity	Reciprocality or overlap
"All"-type statements	• All cats are mammals. • Cats are mammals. • Every cat is a mammal. • Anything that is a cat is a mammal. • All non-mammals are non-cats.	• All cats are not birds. • All birds are not whales.	n/a
"Only"-type statements	• Only mammals are cats. • A thing is a cat only if it is a mammal.	• Only things that are not birds are cats. • Only things that are not cats are birds.	n/a
"No"-type statements	• No cat is not a mammal. • Nothing is a cat unless it is a mammal.	• No cats are birds. • No birds are cats. • Nothing that is a cat is a bird. • Nothing that is a bird is a cat.	n/a

Exhibit 5.5 (*Cont'd*)

	Mutual inclusivity	Mutual exclusivity	Reciprocality or overlap
"If...then"-type statements	• If anything is a cat, (then) it is a mammal. • If anything is not a mammal, (then) it is not a cat.	• If anything is a cat, (then) it is not a bird. • If anything is a bird, (then) it is not a cat.	n/a
"Some"-type statements	n/a	n/a	• Some mammals live in the sea. • Some things that live in the sea are mammals.
"Most"-type statements	n/a	n/a	• Most mammals do not live in the sea. • Most things that live in the sea are not mammals.

Testing Logic-based Reasoning

Tip #42: Be careful not to reverse the flow of "If ... then" statements. "If A, then B" is not the same as "If B, then A." This is known in logic as the fallacy of affirming the consequent.

PROBLEM 31   CHEMIST

"If someone is a chemist, he or she is a scientist. Ms. Zubrinski is a scientist. Therefore, she is a chemist."

Which of the following best explains why the argument above is invalid?

A) Someone cannot be a chemist without being a scientist, so someone cannot be a scientist without being a chemist.

B) Someone cannot be a chemist without being a scientist, but someone can be a scientist without being a chemist.

C) Someone cannot be a scientist without being a chemist, but someone can be a chemist without being a scientist.

D) Someone can be a scientist without being a chemist, and a chemist without being a scientist.

E) Someone can be either a scientist or a chemist, but not one without being the other.

Tip #43: The statement "If A, then B" leads to the logical inference "If not B, then not A." This is known in logic as the contrapositive.

PROBLEM 32   INTRICATE PLOTS

The ability to create intricate plots is one of the essential gifts of the scriptwriter. Strong plot development ensures that eventual moviegoers will be intellectually and emotionally satisfied by the story. If scriptwriting is to remain a significant art form, its practitioners must continue to craft intricate plots.

The author of the argument above would most probably agree with which one of the following statements?

A) If a script has an intricate plot, it must necessarily be a significant art form.

B) A script without an intricate plot will never become a blockbuster movie.

C) If a script does not have an intricate plot, it will probably not be a significant art form.

D) Scriptwriting is the most likely art form to become a significant art form.

E) A scriptwriter must craft multiple plots within his or her scripts.

Tip #44: The statement "If A, then B" does not equal "If not A, then not B." This is known in logic as the fallacy of denying the antecedent.

PROBLEM 33   CAMPUS PUB

"During final exam week, campus pub sells a lot of beer. But it isn't final exam week, so our campus pub must not be selling much beer."

Which of the following is logically most similar to the argument above?

A) When people are happy, they smile, but no one is smiling, so it must be that no one is happy.

B) When people are happy, they smile; our family members are happy, so they must be smiling.

C) When people are happy, they smile, but one can smile and not be happy.

D) When people are happy, they smile, but no one is happy, so no one is smiling.

E) When people are not happy, they do not smile; our family members are smiling, so they must not be unhappy.

Tip #45: One way to think about an "If...then" statement in the form of "If A, then B" is that just because A leads to B does not mean that C, D, or E could not also lead to B.

PROBLEM 34 BALCONY

If your apartment is above the fifth floor, it has a balcony.

The statement above can be logically deduced from which of the following statements?

A) No apartments on the fifth floor have balconies.
B) An apartment does not have a balcony unless the apartment is above the fifth floor.
C) All apartments above the fifth floor have balconies.
D) All balconies are built for apartments above the fifth floor.
E) Balconies are not built for apartments below the fifth floor.

Tip #46: Necessary conditions are not the same as sufficient conditions. The statement "A person needs water to remain healthy" does not mean that water alone is enough to keep a person healthy. Water is a necessary but not sufficient condition for someone to remain healthy.

PROBLEM 35 GLOBAL WARMING

JACQUES: If we want to stop global warming, we must pass legislation to reduce fossil fuel emissions.

PIERRE: That's not true. It will take a lot more than passing legislation aimed at reducing fossil fuel emissions to stop global warming.

Pierre's response is inadequate because he mistakenly believes that what Jacques has said is that

A) Passing legislation to reduce fossil fuel emissions is necessary to reduce global warming.
B) Only the passing of legislation to reduce fossil fuel emissions is capable of stopping global warming.

C) If global warming is to be stopped, legislation to reduce fossil fuel emissions must be passed.

D) Passing legislation to reduce fossil fuel emissions is enough to stop global warming.

E) Global warming will not be stopped merely by passing legislation to reduce fossil fuel emissions.

Tip #47: The statement "If A, then B" does not equal "Only As are Bs." For example, the statement "If one wants to make a good salad, one should use tomatoes" should not be interpreted to mean that only tomatoes are necessary to make a good salad.

PROBLEM 36   SALES

DEBRA: To be a good salesperson, one must be friendly.

TOM: That's not so. It takes much more than friendliness to make a good salesperson.

Tom has understood Debra's statement to mean that

A) Being friendly is the most important characteristic of being a good salesperson.

B) If a person is a good salesperson, he or she will be friendly.

C) A salesperson only needs to be friendly in order to be a good salesperson.

D) Most good salespersons are friendly people even though not all friendly people are good salespersons.

E) If a person isn't friendly, he or she will not make a good salesperson.

Tip #48: The statement "Every A is a B" does not equal "Only As are Bs." For example, the statement "Every cat is a mammal" should not be interpreted to mean that "Only cats are mammals."

Problem 37 Football

MARIE: Every person on the Brazilian World Cup football team is a great player.

BETH: What? The Italian World Cup football team has some of the best players in the world.

Beth's reply suggests that she has misunderstood Marie's remark to mean that

A) Only Brazilian World Cup team players are great players.

B) Marie believes that the Brazilian World Cup football team is the best overall football team.

C) The Italian World Cup football team consists of less-than-great players.

D) The Brazilian World Cup football team is likely to defeat the Italian World Cup football team should they meet in match play.

E) Individual Brazilian World Cup team players will play as well as a unit as will the Italian World Cup team players.

Tip #49: "All" statements imply inclusivity; "some" statements imply crossover; "no" statements imply exclusivity.

Problem 38 Medical Hierarchy

All surgeons are doctors.

Some researchers are surgeons.

All doctors are medically licensed.

No student is medically licensed.

If all the statements above are true, which one of the following cannot be true?

A) No doctors are researchers.
B) Some surgeons are doctors but not researchers.
C) Some researchers are doctors but not surgeons.
D) Some surgeons are medically licensed but not researchers.
E) Some researchers are neither surgeons nor medically licensed.

Tip #50: Whereas "some" statements imply reciprocality, "most" statements do not necessarily imply reciprocality.

Problem 39 Valley High

Based on information obtained from the Admissions and Registrar's Office of Valley High School, curriculum advisors observed the following enrollment trends for the semester in progress.

No math student is studying French.
All physics students study math.
Most math students are also studying English.
Some English students also study creative writing.

If the statements above are true, which of the following must be false?

A) Some creative writing students also study French.
B) All physics students also study English.
C) All math students also study physics.
D) Some, but not most English students also study math.
E) Some physics students also study French.

Appendixes

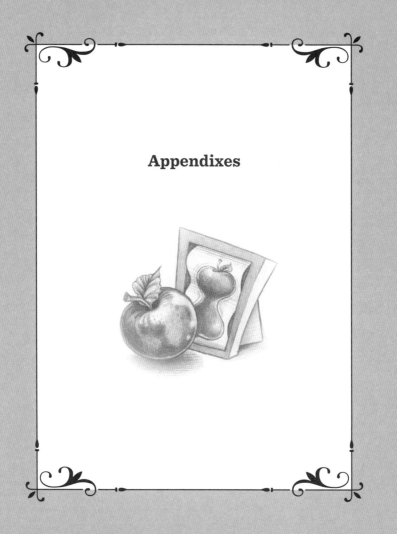

Nothing hath an uglier look to us than reason, when it is not of our side.

—HALIFAX

Appendix I—Summary of Reasoning Tips 1 to 50

Chapter 1: Perception and Mindset

Tip #1: Selective perception is the tendency to see the world the way we would like it to be rather than how it really is. The sound thinker suspends judgment and is not unduly influenced by stereotypes, prejudices, isolated experiences, or preconceived notions.

Tip #2: Think of mindsets as divided into four basic types: Analysts, Idealists, Realists, and Synthesists. These mindsets can be further contrasted based on levels of practicality and emotional attachment.

Chapter 2: Creative Thinking

Tip #3: Creative thinking is "backdoor" thinking.

Tip #4: Convergent thinking focuses the mind; divergent thinking opens the mind.

Tip #5: The devil's advocate technique imposes objectivity and compels divergent thinking.

Tip #6: Not challenging the obvious, evaluating ideas too quickly, and fear of looking the fool—these are the three greatest creativity inhibitors.

Tip #7: Keep a mental list of idea "killers" and idea "growers."

Tip #8: Brainstorming has rules: quantity of ideas is preferred, wacky ideas are welcomed, delayed evaluation is mandatory, and "hitchhiking" is encouraged.

Tip #9: Consider whether a problem is really the problem. Think in terms of redefining the problem.

Tip #10: In selling creative ideas, most people are moved more by the depth of a person's conviction and commitment than they are by the details of a logical presentation.

Chapter 3: Decision Making

Tip #11: Pros-and-cons analysis may be illustrated using a "T-Account," with pros on one side and cons on the other side.

Tip #12: A matrix is a useful tool to summarize data that can be contrasted across two variables and sorted into four distinct outcomes.

Tip #13: Decision-event trees are a way to represent graphically the multiple outcomes involved in a decision scenario.

Tip #14: The end branches of a probability tree must total to 1, which is equal to the aggregate of all individual probabilities.

Tip #15: Weighted ranking is a tool for finding solutions using a weighted average. To calculate weighted average, we multiply each event by its associated weight and total the results. In the case of probabilities, we multiply each event by its respective probability and total the results.

Tip #16: Utility analysis takes into account desirability of outcomes, which may be different from monetary payoffs.

Tip #17: Sunk costs are irrelevant to future decision making.

Tip #18: For the purposes of hypothesis testing, the minimum requirement for causal inference is evaluation using a "two-way" table.

Tip #19: The Prisoner's Dilemma provides an example of how cooperation is superior to competition.

Chapter 4: Analyzing Arguments

Tip #20: Evidence + Assumption = Conclusion. The assumption is the glue that holds the evidence to the conclusion.

Tip #21: There are effectively two ways to attack an argument: attack the evidence or attack the assumption(s).

Tip #22: The five most common critical reasoning errors that people make include: comparing "apples with oranges," overgeneralizing on the basis of small samples, ignoring relevant evidence, confusing cause and effect, and failing to anticipate bottlenecks when plans are put into action.

Tip #23: Watch for "scope shifts," which occur when one term is substituted for another as an argument unfolds.

Tip #24: Changes in the way words are defined destroy the ability to make valid comparisons.

Tip #25: If a situation involves a "survey," check to see if the survey is based on a sample which is both quantitatively and qualitatively representative.

Tip #26: Representativeness assumptions are based on the idea that some smaller "thing" is representative of the larger whole.

Tip #27: Broadly speaking, representativeness assumptions occur anytime that we argue from the particular to the general.

Tip #28: Check to see whether evidence has been handpicked to support a claim being made. Otherwise we may fall victim to "proof by selected instances."

Tip #29: "Evidence omitted" may hold the key to determining an argument's validity.

Tip #30: Correlation does not equal causation.

Tip #31: Cause-and-effect assumptions are grounded in the idea that because one event follows another in time, the first of the two events is the cause and the second is the effect.

Tip #32: When tackling cause-and-effect scenarios, think first in terms of alternative causal explanations. If the argument states that A is causing B, then check to see that another cause, namely C, is not instead causing B.

Tip #33: A more complex form of alternative explanation occurs when two effects result from a single cause. Thus, if an argument suggests that A is causing B, consider the possibility that another cause, namely C, could be causing both A and B.

Tip #34: If A is thought to be causing B, the idea that B is causing A is called reverse causation and casts serious doubt on the notion that A is really causing B.

Tip #35: Test the opposite scenario—if you hear that a full moon causes the crime rate to rise, always ask what the crime rate is like when the moon is not full.

Tip #36: Theory may be divorced from practice. Plans may not equal completed action. Do not assume that plans will be implemented without a hitch.

Tip #37: "Can" does not equal "will." The ability to do something should not imply application of that ability, whether due to choice or neglect.

Tip #38: One way to uncover implementation assumptions is to anticipate bottlenecks.

Tip #39: An argument may depend on the assumption that a person or organization is aware of a pre-existing fact, situation, or condition.

Tip #40: Searching for something does not guarantee that we'll recognize it once we've found it. The ability to accurately identify that which we are seeking to find may be a key assumption.

Tip #41: Always look for potentially vague terms in an argument and ask for or seek clarification.

Chapter 5: Mastering Logic

Tip #42: Be careful not to reverse the flow of "If ... then" statements. "If A, then B" is not the same as "If B, then A." This is known in logic as the fallacy of affirming the consequent.

Tip #43: The statement "If A, then B" leads to the logical inference "If not B, then not A." This is known in logic as the contrapositive.

Tip #44: The statement "If A, then B" does not equal "If not A, then not B." This is known in logic as the fallacy of denying the antecedent.

Tip #45: One way to think about an "If ... then" statement in the form of "If A, then B" is that just because A leads to B does not mean that C, D, or E could not also lead to B.

Tip #46: Necessary conditions are not the same as sufficient conditions. The statement "A person needs water to remain healthy" does not mean that water alone is enough to keep a person healthy. Water is a necessary but not sufficient condition for someone to remain healthy.

Tip #47: The statement "If A, then B" does not equal "Only As are Bs." For example, the statement "If one wants to make a good salad, one should use tomatoes" should not be interpreted to mean that only tomatoes are necessary to make a good salad.

Tip #48: The statement "Every A is a B" does not equal "Only As are Bs." For example, the statement "Every cat is a mammal" should not be interpreted to mean that "Only cats are mammals."

Tip #49: "All" statements imply inclusivity; "some" statements imply crossover; "no" statements imply exclusivity.

Tip #50: Whereas "some" statements imply reciprocality, "most" statements do not necessarily imply reciprocality.

Appendix II—Fallacious Reasoning

A traditional approach to argumentation involves studying common types of fallacious reasoning. This method is consistent with what a person might encounter in an introductory logic course in college or university.

It is valuable to recognize fallacious types of reasoning and defend against them. One benefit of studying fallacious reasoning is to avoid unknowingly constructing fallacious arguments. "Feeling" that an argument is fallacious is one thing; being able to specifically identify why something is fallacious is quite another. This difference is analogous to feeling sick but not knowing why, as opposed to seeing a doctor and finding out exactly what the reason is.

The fallacies presented in this section are divided into four major groupings, including: (1) fallacies based on language; (2) fallacies based on "bad" evidence; (3) fallacies based on flawed assumptions;

and (4) fallacies found in deductive logic. Each fallacy is accompanied by a brief description of the fallacy and at least one key example to illustrate it.

The following are fallacies based on language:

EQUIVOCATION

The fallacy of equivocation occurs when someone uses a word or phrase that has two different meanings depending on its context.

> *"Gambling should be legalized everywhere because it is something we can't avoid. It is part of life itself. People gamble every time they get behind the wheel of their cars or say their wedding vows."*

The word "gambling" is used in two different contexts, creating ambiguity or equivocation.

Equivocation can even occur in the revered domain of syllogistic logic.

> *"All lemons are yellow.*
> *This car is a lemon.*
> *Therefore, this car is yellow."*

Since lemon has two different meanings—the first referring to a fruit and the second meaning "inferior" or "defective"—a case of fallacious reasoning arises: the conclusion does not follow logically from the premises.

DISTINCTION WITHOUT A DIFFERENCE

The fallacy of distinction without a difference occurs when a person argues that his or her position is different from a previous one by means of careful distinction of language. However, even though the words chosen are different, they are in substance identical to the ones already used.

> *"I didn't lie. I just stretched the truth a bit."*

What is the difference between lying and stretching the truth?

The following are fallacies based on "bad" evidence:

HASTY GENERALIZATION
The fallacy of hasty generalization occurs when a conclusion is reached based on too small a sample size or on a sample that is unrepresentative.

> *"I have been to Phoenix three times and each time it has rained. Phoenix sure does get a lot of rain."*

CIRCULAR REASONING
The fallacy of circular reasoning occurs when a conclusion is based on a premise (a piece of evidence) which in turn is based on the conclusion.

> *"Mr. Weeble's desk is always messy because he's incompetent. A messy desk is the sign of a cluttered mind, and this tells us something: he simply can't get the job done."*

The argument above effectively states: "incompetence leads to a messy desk and a messy desk leads to work not getting done (i.e., to incompetence)."

FALLACY OF NEGATIVE PROOF
The fallacy of negative proof occurs when a claim is deemed true because it is not proven false, or false because it is not proven true. For example, the fact that no one has found evidence that Atlantis (the fabled lost continent) existed does not prove that Atlantis did not exist.

> *"Because no intern in our office has ever complained about his or her salary, we can be confident that interns in our office are satisfied with their wages."*

AD HOMINEM
The ad hominem fallacy consists in attacking the person, often in a personal or abusive way, rather than attacking the argument or claim being made.

> *"How can you let Sheila give you marital advice? Don't you know she spent some time in jail for mail fraud?"*

POISONING THE WELL

The fallacy of poisoning the well consists of rejecting an opponent's argument because of the opponent's background, particularly as it relates to nationality, race, gender, or geography.

> *"How can what you say be credible? You're from Sydney, and of course you think Sydney is a better city than Melbourne."*

TU QUOQUE

The tu quoque fallacy consists of refusing to accept an opponent's stance or position because the opponent is guilty of these very same charges.

FATHER: *You shouldn't drink, son. Drinking hurts your liver, and being drunk and stupid is no way to go through life.*

SON: *Dad, isn't that a gin and tonic in your hand?*

Even though the boy's father is drinking, it doesn't mean the father's point is without merit.

RED HERRING

The red herring fallacy consists in attempting to hide a weakness in an argument by drawing attention away from the real issue and emphasizing a side issue.

> *(Boss to employee): "Don't tell me about low wages. When I was your age, I was making only a hundred dollars a week."*

The fact that this employee's boss made less when she or he was young is irrelevant to a concerned employee seeking a wage increase.

ASSIGNING IRRELEVANT GOALS OR FUNCTIONS

The fallacy of assigning irrelevant goals or functions consists of rejecting a policy or course of action because it fails to satisfy certain goals or objectives that it was never intended to achieve.

> PETER: *Do you really think that studying logic is going to help us solve the world's problems?*
>
> TIFFANY: *No, probably not.*
>
> PETER: *Then why are you wasting your time studying it?*

WISHFUL THINKING

The fallacy of wishful thinking occurs when one assumes that just because one wishes something to be true (or false), it will therefore be the case.

> *"Forget all about our team's rather lackluster performance this season. Our football team is going to defeat the defending champions in the first round of the playoffs. All of our players believe in themselves and are determined to pull off an upset victory."*

FALLACY OF TRADITION

The fallacy of tradition consists in trying to persuade someone based on history, heritage, or reverence rather than relying on the strength of the evidence.

> *"Tim, you can't be serious about going to Annapolis! Your family has been and always will be Army—your father, brother, grandfather, and uncle. It's West Point for you, my friend."*

APPEAL TO PUBLIC OPINION

The fallacy of appeal to public opinion occurs when an idea or position is accepted because a great number of people also accept or support it.

> *"I'm going to vote 'yes' on the proposed tax bill amendment. According to a recent poll, more than two-thirds of the registered voters under the age of twenty-five support it."*

APPEAL TO PITY

The fallacy of appeal to pity consists of using sympathy to persuade rather than relying on the strength of the evidence presented.

> *(Sheila to John) "You have to donate to the orphanage. It is bad enough that children will never know who their real parents are, let alone being deprived of the basic necessities of life."*

The following are fallacies based on flawed assumptions:

FALSE ALTERNATIVES

The fallacy of false alternatives involves assuming that one of two alternatives is correct. These alternatives are usually extreme and fail to acknowledge middle ground. The fallacy of false alternatives is also referred to as the "either-or" fallacy or "black-and-white" fallacy.

> *"If you're not for free trade, you must be for protectionism."*

FALLACY OF THE GOLDEN MEAN

The fallacy of the golden mean consists in believing that the middle option is best because it is the point between two extremes. This is also called the fallacy of moderation.

"Junior high school teachers believe students should follow a fixed course curriculum. The parents of junior high school students believe that students should be allowed to pick their own courses. The best solution is to combine the wishes of teachers and parents."

FALLACY OF COMPOSITION

The fallacy of composition consists in believing that what is true for the parts must therefore be true for the whole.

"Brad is a fine young man. Janet is a fine young woman. They'll make a wonderful couple."

As marriage is deemed to be more than the sum of its parts by virtue of the couple's relationship in the marital whole, the result might be something more or less than the "parts" added together.

FALLACY OF DIVISION

The fallacy of division involves believing that what is true for the whole is also true for the individual parts. For example, just because the New Zealand rugby team is a great team, this does not mean all players on the New Zealand rugby team are great players.

"Because a car is a heavy object, all components that go into making a car are heavy in weight."

FALLACY OF THE CONTINUUM

The fallacy of the continuum is the result of believing that small or incremental differences can be ignored because they are inconsequential on a larger scale.

"Try building your vocabulary by studying one new word each day. Take a medium-sized dictionary and start at the beginning. Learn one word one day and another the next.

Eventually, you will have gone cover to cover, and, more
importantly, you will have learned almost every important
word in the English language. How many people can boast
of that?"

Incorrect Attack on a Generalization

The fallacy of incorrect attack on a generalization consists in believing that a generalization is open to attack because a single exception can be cited. For example, a theatre sign stating that those under eighteen years of age should not enter a theatre does not mean that parents carrying their seven-month-old baby should not be permitted to enter.

STUDENT #1: *It is a well-known fact that smoking shortens*
your life expectancy.

STUDENT #2: *Yeah, well then how do you explain the fact that*
my great grandfather smokes a pack a day and
he's rockin' into his nineties?

Finding an exception to a generalization does not undermine the generalization—a generalization is merely a generalization.

Distortion

The fallacy of distortion consists in twisting an opponent's point of view or claim, thereby making it easier to attack.

PROPONENT: *The only way to increase education in developing*
countries is to have materials, and this means
textbooks.

OPPONENT: *What you're saying is that you couldn't care less*
about depleting our forests to provide paper for,
God knows, how many more textbooks.

FAULTY ANALOGY

The fallacy of faulty analogy consists in believing that because two things are alike (or unlike) in one or more aspects they are alike (or unlike) in one or more other aspects.

> *"When it comes to artificial lures, the Rappala artificial minnow has worked like a charm for me. I've used it every day this summer to catch small mouth bass and can't wait to try it when going trout fishing in the fall."*

CAUSE AND EFFECT (CAUSAL OVERSIMPLIFICATION)

The fallacy of causal oversimplification occurs when one assumes that a particular cause is responsible for a given effect.

> *"I have heard that rich people work hard. I am going to work hard and get rich."*

Hard work will no doubt contribute to someone's getting rich, but it is probably only one of several contributing factors. It is wrong to assume that hard work alone is a sufficient condition for becoming rich.

DOMINO FALLACY

The domino fallacy consists in assuming that because one event may cause another to occur it will also cause a series of future events to occur. This fallacy is also referred to as the chain reaction fallacy.

> *"I don't see a problem with giving the homeless a free meal, but a free meal leads to free clothing, and if we're not careful, free accommodation. Pretty soon we'll be giving them a guaranteed annual salary as well."*

GAMBLER'S FALLACY

The gambler's fallacy consists in concluding that a future event's chance or probability is altered based on a previous event's outcome, even though the two are independent events with absolutely no influence on one another.

> *(Parents conversing with their doctor): "Because we already have three boys, the odds greatly favor our having a baby girl."*

The result of one birth has absolutely no influence (almost no influence, biologically speaking) on the gender of future offspring. The odds are still 50–50.

FALLACY OF FALSE PRECISION

The fallacy of false precision consists in making a claim with a level of mathematical precision that is likely impossible to obtain.

> *"One out of every four people in Shakespeare's day did not actually like Shakespeare's plays."*

It is unlikely that such a precise figure could be obtained, particularly during that time period.

The following are fallacies found in deductive logic:

FALLACY OF AFFIRMING THE CONSEQUENT

The fallacy of affirming the consequent assumes that in an "If A, then B" scenario, the opposite, "If B, then A," is also true. This is sometimes called the fallacy of false conversion.

> *"Whenever I go on vacation, I feel relaxed. I feel relaxed, so I must be on vacation."*

The absurdity of this fallacy can be seen by showing those times that one is relaxed other than being on vacation: When I'm at home, I feel relaxed . . . When I'm at dinner, I feel relaxed . . . When I'm with friends, I feel relaxed.

FALLACY OF DENYING THE ANTECEDENT

The fallacy of denying the antecedent assumes that in an "If A, then B" scenario, it is also true that "If not A, then not B."

> *"Whenever it rains the ground gets wet. It didn't rain last night so the ground can't be wet."*

For all we know, the sprinkler system may have been turned on, causing the ground to be wet.

For a review of both of the preceding fallacies, refer to the discussion of "If . . . then"–type statements on pages 138–141.

Appendix III—Avoiding Improper Inferences

Developing the mindset to master critical reasoning requires knowing where to "draw the line" between inferable and non-inferable statements. First, let's contrast the terms inference and assumption. An assumption is an unstated premise which is an integral component of any argument—it is the missing link needed to make an argument work. An inference is a logical extension—a logically inferable statement based on an argument, statement, or passage.

In everyday life we make loose inferences. We make inferences based on what is "most probably true." For example, the statement, "It's been raining a lot lately," begs the inference "umbrella sales are up." The statement, "The weather's getting colder," begs the inference that "ice cream sales are down." But these are not logically inferable. What is "logically inferable" is a much firmer, tighter noose than what is "most probably true."

Take the following argument: "Buy our product. It's the cheapest in the market." The conclusion is "buy our product." The evidence is "it's the cheapest in the market." The assumption is "price is the dominant factor in a purchasing decision." The statement "other products in the market are more expensive" is not an assumption but an inference—a logically inferable statement based on the argument.

PROBLEM 40   LITTLE ITALY

Antonio is a well-known Italian connoisseur operating the Little Italy restaurant in Devon City. Not only do three out of every four food and beverage consultants recommend his Italian restaurant, but a survey by the city's Food and Beverage Association shows that his restaurant is unsurpassed by any other Italian restaurant in the city. The proof is in the eating. Antonio's customers prefer his style of Italian cooking by a ratio of 2 to 1.

Which of the statements below are logically inferable based on the brief passage about the Little Italy restaurant above? Answers can be found on pages 240–241.

1. Antonio's restaurant Little Italy is regarded by the city's Food and Beverage Association as the best Italian restaurant in the city.

   ❑ True   ❑ False

2. Antonio enjoys preparing Italian food.

   ❑ True   ❑ False

3. Food and beverage consultants recommend Antonio's restaurant more than they do other Italian restaurants in the city.

   ❑ True   ❑ False

4. Antonio's customers prefer his style of Italian cooking to that of other comparable Italian restaurants.

   ❑ True   ❑ False

5. Spaghetti is one of the restaurant's most requested dishes.

   ❑ True   ❑ False

6. Antonio uses high-quality ingredients in the dishes served in his restaurant.

   ❑ True   ❑ False

7. The Little Italy restaurant is a profitable business.

   ❑ True   ❑ False

8. If Antonio moved to another city, he would also be able to establish himself as a well-known Italian connoisseur.

❏ True ❏ False

9. Prices for food in Little Italy are relatively expensive.

❏ True ❏ False

10. Antonio has spent much time acquiring his reputation as an Italian connoisseur.

❏ True ❏ False

Appendix IV—Analogies

Analogies are one of the most underrated tools for creative thinking and reasoning. Analogies help define the relationships between two or more things. Identifying simple relationships begins with an understanding of what types of potential relationships exist. Although analogies exist across the four primary symbolic systems which we use to communicate—words, numbers, pictures, and music—this appendix concerns itself only with verbal analogies. Ten major categories of verbal analogies include: synonym, antonym, part to whole, part to part, cause and effect, degree, sequence, function or purpose, characteristic, and association.

Type of Analogy:

1. **SYNONYM**

   Definition: Synonyms are words or phrases that are similar in meaning.

   Example: HELP : ASSIST

   Both "help" and "assist" share similar meanings.

2. **ANTONYM**

   Definition: Antonyms are words or phrases that are opposite in meaning.

   Example: OPTIMISTIC : PESSIMISTIC

Optimistic means "expecting the best"; this is opposed to pessimistic, which means "expecting the worst."

3. **Part to Whole**

   Definition: Something smaller is compared to something larger (or vice-versa).

   Example: BRANCH : TREE

   A branch is a smaller part of a whole tree.

4. **Part to Part**

   Definition: Something which is a part of a whole is compared to something else which is itself part of another whole.

   Example: FOOT : HAND

   Foot is part of the leg as hand is part of the arm.

5. **Cause and Effect**

   Definition: Something that creates a situation (called the "cause") is matched with the result of that cause (called the "effect").

   Example: FIRE : SMOKE

   A fire causes smoke (fire is the cause; smoke is the effect).

6. **Degree**

   Definition: Shows an increase or decrease in the intensity of two items.

   Example: HAPPY : ECSTATIC

   Ecstatic means extremely happy.

7. **SEQUENCE**

Definition: Shows the progression from one thing to another.
Example: SPRING : SUMMER

Summer is the season that follows spring (or spring is the season that comes before summer).

8. **FUNCTION OR PURPOSE**

Definition: Shows how something is used, how it functions, or what purpose it has.
Example: SCISSORS : CUT

Scissors are used to cut things.

9. **CHARACTERISTIC**

Definition: Describes something in terms of one of its dominant characteristics (usually an adjective).
Example: MONK : TOLERANT

A monk can be described as tolerant.

10. **ASSOCIATION**

Definition: Describes a connection between two words based on association or common understanding.
Example: FRANCE : EIFFEL TOWER

The Eiffel Tower is associated with France.

PROBLEM 41 ANALOGY EXERCISE

Choose the answer—A through D—which best completes each analogy. Also, identify the type of analogy presented by choosing from the list at the top of the next page. Answers can be found on pages 241–243.

Types of Analogy:

Synonym

Antonym

Part to Whole

Part to Part

Cause and Effect

Degree

Sequence

Function or Purpose

Characteristic

Association

1. RED : PINK :: BLACK :
   A) beige
   B) white
   C) gray
   D) dark

2. HEAT : RADIATOR :: BREEZE :
   A) sea
   B) wind
   C) shade
   D) fan

3. BIG : LARGE :: WIDE :
   A) high
   B) broad
   C) long
   D) small

4. DOG : CAT :: CROCODILE :
   A) reptile
   B) hippopotamus
   C) lizard
   D) elephant

5. FLOWER : BOUQUET :: LINK :
   A) gold
   B) steel
   C) orchard
   D) chain

6. TOMORROW : YESTERDAY :: FUTURE :
   A) present
   B) past
   C) ago
   D) today

7. HERO : VALOR :: HERETIC :
   A) dissent
   B) bravado
   C) reverence
   D) discretion

8. PRESENT : BIRTHDAY :: REWARD :
   A) accomplishment
   B) punishment
   C) medal
   D) money

9. SKY : GROUND :: CEILING :
   A) floor
   B) roof
   C) to
   D) plaster

10. MONEY : BANK :: KNOWLEDGE :
   A) intelligence
   B) reading
   C) graduation
   D) books

Appendix V—The Ten Classic Trade-offs

Reasoning can at times be viewed in terms of polar opposites and trade-offs. As children, we learn the simplicity of remembering things by recognizing opposing traits and characteristics, and as adults, we continue to grapple with ideas expressed in contradictory ways.

Consider the following pairs of well-known quotes:

He who hesitates is lost.
Haste makes waste.

Nothing ventured, nothing gained.
Better safe than sorry.

Out of sight, out of mind.
Absence makes the heart grow fonder.

Many hands make light work.
Too many cooks spoil the broth.

Certain trade-offs also recur in the realm of reasoning and decision making. Familiarity with such trade-offs speeds recognition of core issues.

A summary of the 10 classic trade-offs presented here includes:

1. Breadth vs. Depth
2. Control vs. Chance
3. Individual vs. Collective
4. Means vs. Ends
5. Quantity vs. Quality
6. Short-term vs. Long-term
7. Specific vs. General
8. Subjective vs. Objective
9. Theory vs. Practice
10. Tradition vs. Change

1. Breadth vs. Depth Trade-off

Inevitably, each person has experienced this trade-off in terms of the "depth" versus "breadth" of his or her academic, professional, or personal experience. Do we have a lot of one thing or a little of a lot? In terms of academics, should we focus deeply on our studies or should we engage in lots of school activities as well? In commerce, a factory might choose to produce lots of one type of product or smaller quantities of a diverse number of products. In terms of our personal investment strategy, do we put all our money in one type of investment (depth) or do we spread our money over two or more different investments (breadth)?

2. Control vs. Chance Trade-off

The more a situation is subject to control, the less it is subject to chance. The more a situation is left to chance, the less it is under control. The "nature versus nurture" controversy is a famous example of the control versus chance trade-off. Does heredity play a dominant role in personality or does upbringing and environment? Here nature is the "chance" element in personality development and nurture is the "control" element. Although many people believe in a middle-of-the-road approach, the core issue is one viewed in terms of polarity or mutual opposition.

3. Individual vs. Collective Trade-off

What is more important, the individual or the group? By upholding individual rights or freedoms, do we not sacrifice collective rights and freedoms (and vice versa)? This apparent trade-off is the focal point around which pivots the constitution of virtually every developed country.

4. Means vs. Ends Trade-off

"Means" are the ways or approaches while "ends" are the outcomes or results. Typically two people might disagree in terms of the means but share the same end. A simple real-life example involves two people debating about which route (means) to take to get to a single downtown location (end). Sometimes, we disagree in terms of the end but agree on the means. Suppose we have decided to spend bonus money on a vacation but are deliberating about where to go. Here is a classic situation of sharing the same means (i.e., spending money to go on vacation) but not knowing what the ends should be (i.e., vacation destination).

5. Quantity vs. Quality Trade-off

The quantity versus quality trade-off appears frequently in everyday life. Rarely do we demand more and, at the same time, realistically expect better quality as well. For example, in terms of a price and quantity trade-off, a lower price generally means more quantity and lower quality, while a higher price means higher quality but lower quantity.

6. Short-term vs. Long-term Trade-off

Sometimes the only difference between two opposing points of view is a difference in time frames. Two people, for example, might equally believe in the potential benefits of space exploration, but disagree as to whether it's a priority worth pursuing in the short-run.

7. Specific vs. General Trade-off

"Specific" is like seeing the trees, and "general" is like seeing the forest. A startup company will likely have more success as a niche player (known for selling a specific product or service), but as it grows it will become a generalist (known for selling a number of products or services). Perhaps you know people who are good with details but poor with the bigger picture; others are good with the bigger picture but poor with details. The fictional fellow James Bond is a rare specimen indeed—one who is both detail-minded ("can see the trees") and a generalist ("can see the forest")!

How does the breadth versus depth trade-off differ from a specific versus general trade-off? Specific versus general is about scope. Specific means we have a narrow scope; general means we have a broad scope. Breadth versus depth is about variety. Breadth means we have a lot of variety; depth means we have less variety and more constancy.

Take an example from photography. We decide to snap some photos of a large summer garden. In our role as a generalist, we stand back and take pictures of the whole of the garden. The more pictures we take of the whole garden from different angles, the more breadth our photography collection will have. The more pictures of the whole garden from a similar angle, the more depth we'll have.

In our role as a specialist, we advance for close-up shots. By taking close-ups of a few select flowers from many different angles, we add breadth to our collection. By taking lots of close-up shots of a few select flowers from one particular angle, we add depth to our photo collection.

8. Subjective vs. Objective Trade-off

Subjective means that something is based on personal experience, feeling, or opinion. Objective means that something is not based on personal experience, feeling, or opinion—it is impartial and based in fact. The subjective versus objective trade-off has many faces. These include: art versus science, emotion versus logic, and passion versus intellect. It is ostensibly impossible to maintain subjectivity and objectivity simultaneously.

9. Theory vs. Practice Trade-off

Perhaps the easiest way to think of a theory versus practice trade-off is to view it in terms of schooling versus work experience. Schooling is equated with theory and work experience with practice. It is generally assumed that a given situation involves more of one of these two things to the neglect of the other.

10. Tradition vs. Change Trade-off

The past hails tradition and the future hails change. In everyday life, we might argue for a return to tradition, as in the case of family values or work ethic. In other situations, a person will push for change and opt for a different set of values or work ethic. Culture and tradition are almost always in conflict with change and modernization. In America, the right to own and/or carry handguns and automatic weapons is supported in large measure because the American Constitution ("tradition") provides for the right to bear arms. Others, who are opposed to the proliferation of guns and the ease at which individuals can gain access to handguns and automatic weapons, argue that the American Constitution needs to be amended ("change").

PROBLEM 42 MATCHING EXERCISE

Which trade-offs are showcased in the scenarios below? Place the number in the appropriate box, thereby matching the problem number—1 through 10—with the trade-off—A through J—which best describes the subject matter contained in the narratives. Answers can be found on pages 243–246.

- ❑ A. Breadth vs. Depth
- ❑ B. Control vs. Chance
- ❑ C. Individual vs. Collective
- ❑ D. Means vs. Ends
- ❑ E. Quantity vs. Quality
- ❑ F. Short-term vs. Long-term
- ❑ G. Specific vs. General
- ❑ H. Subjective vs. Objective
- ❑ I. Theory vs. Practice
- ❑ J. Tradition vs. Change

1. Fossil Fuels

BRENDA: In the long run, fossil fuels, including oil, coal, and even gas, will be exhausted, and the major practical alternative will be solar energy. Therefore, we should develop that option in the remaining time.

BOB: I disagree. It would be foolish to switch to energy generated from crude solar energy systems, and it is unnecessary to do so, when the supply of oil, coal, and especially gas are more than adequate for our current needs.

2. Miracle Tablets

One Miracle tablet contains twice the pain reliever found in regular aspirin. A consumer will have to take two aspirin to get the relief provided by one Miracle tablet. And since a bottle of Miracle costs the same as a bottle of regular aspirin, consumers can be expected to switch to Miracle.

3. Pirates

International anti-piracy laws, restricting the unauthorized duplication of music CDs and online downloads, must be more effectively enforced. Effective reinforcement would lead to greater revenues for the music companies that lose millions of dollars each year on illegal copies and downloads. This increase in revenue would stimulate music companies to release a wider range of their prerecorded music. That outcome alone makes rigid enforcement a benefit to music fans who had previously saved money on cheaper, illegal CD copies and downloads.

4. Techies

Dr. Janson's research challenges the conventional wisdom that training unskilled people in a narrow skill like computer programming or accounting will make them upwardly mobile. He claims that a disproportionately small percentage of college graduates with vocational degrees have landed upper-echelon management jobs. According to his research, presidents and CEOs of Fortune 500 companies land and hold upper-echelon jobs because of their broader liberal arts education, which fosters more analytically rigorous minds.

5. Workers

The problem with labor unions today is that their top staffs consist of college-trained lawyers, economists, and labor relations experts who cannot understand the concerns of real workers. The goal of union reform movements should be to recruit top staff members from worker representatives who have come up from the ranks of the industry involved.

6. Sales

During a recent business meeting, management voted unanimously to target increased sales as the best strategy to move the company forward. However, debate ensued as to the best method to achieve this goal. Some key staff members pointed to hiring more salespeople as the key to increasing sales, while others argued that what was needed was a market study to better understand consumer needs.

7. Safe Haven

Wealthy parents living in urban centers, who are increasingly concerned with neighborhood violence such as drive-by shootings, are considering moving to the safety of the suburbs. However, statistics show that the death rate for teenagers in suburban areas is no less than that in urban areas because teenagers living in suburban areas have a higher incidence of suicide as well as death from auto-related accidents.

8. Free Speech

Our government guarantees that we have the right to free speech, and yet this is an illusion. Yelling "Fire!" in a crowded theatre, joking about a bomb while at an airport, or engaging in obscene rants in public—all of these are, in fact, grounds for arrest. Clearly, the government is contradicting its promise of free speech to all.

9. Historians

Today's historians, in an attempt to mimic the work of natural scientists, have adopted the practice of churning out edited laboratory reports, complete with impressive computer data and statistical charts. The best historical writing, however, is produced by bringing imagination and understanding to bear upon evidence from the past. This requires passion, which does not always accord with scientific methods that require the investigator to be detached.

10. Discovery

During the early 1970s, Adam Nordwell, a Native American Chippewa chieftain, arrived by plane in Italy from California. Dressed in full tribal regalia, he descended the steps of the aircraft, and halfway down he stopped and announced: "I proclaim this day the day of discovery of Italy." In a humorous jest, Nordwell was proclaiming possession of Italy for the American Indian people! After all, what right did Columbus have to claim America for Italy, or exercise the right of discovery, when America was already occupied by people who had lived there for centuries?

Appendix VI—Critical Reading and Comprehension

The ability to read while capturing subtleties in written language is an important skill which dovetails with reasoning ability. After reading carefully the passage below, try answering the five questions that follow. This excerpted passage was written by Mortimer J. Adler, author and former chairman of the board of directors of Encyclopedia Britannica and co-founder of The Center for the Study of The Great Ideas.

PROBLEM 43   SAMPLE PASSAGE

1 For more than forty years, a controlling insight in my educational
   philosophy has been the recognition that no one has ever been—
   no one can ever be—educated in school or college. That would be
   the case if our schools and colleges were at their very best, which
5 they certainly are not, and even if the students were among the best
   and the brightest, as well as conscientious in the application of their
   powers. The reason is simply that youth itself—immaturity—is an
   insuperable obstacle to becoming educated. Schooling is for the
   young. Education comes later, usually much later. The very best
10 thing for our schools to do is to prepare the young for continued
   learning in later life by giving them the skills of learning and the
   love of it.

To speak of an educated young person or of a wise young person, rich in the understanding of basic ideas and issues, is as much a
15 contradiction in terms as to speak of a round square. The young can be prepared for education in the years to come, but only mature men and women can become educated, beginning the process in their forties and fifties and reaching some modicum of genuine insight, sound judgment and practical wisdom after they have turned sixty.

20 Those who take this prescription seriously would, of course, be better off if their schooling had given them the intellectual discipline and skill they need to carry it out, and if it also had introduced them to the world of learning with some appreciation of its basic ideas and issues. But even the individual who is fortunate enough to leave
25 school or college with a mind so disciplined, and with an abiding love of learning, would still have a long road to travel before he or she became an educated person. If our schools and colleges were doing their part and adults were doing theirs, all would be well.

However, our schools and colleges are not doing their part
30 because they are trying to do everything else. And adults are not doing their part because most are under the illusion that they had completed their education when they finished their schooling.

Only the person who realizes that mature life is the time to get the education that no young person can ever acquire is at last on
35 the high road to learning. The road is steep and rocky, but it is the high road, open to anyone who has skill in learning and the ultimate goal of all learning in view—understanding the nature of things and mankind's place in the total scheme. An educated person is one who through the travail of his own life has assimilated the ideas
40 that make him representative of his culture, that make him a bearer of its traditions and enable him to contribute to its improvement.

Questions—Choose the best answer based on the previous passage. Answers can be found on pages 247–253.

1. The author's primary purpose in writing this passage is to

   A) Highlight major tenets in educational philosophy in the last 40 years.
   B) Raise public awareness about the need for teachers with training in the liberal arts.
   C) Contrast the words "schooling" and "education."
   D) Suggest that youth stands in the way of one's becoming educated.
   E) Cite the importance of reading with active discussion.

2. According to the passage, the best thing that our schools can do is to

   A) Improve academic instruction at the grassroots level.
   B) Advocate using the word "education" in place of the word "schooling" to better convey to adults the goal of teaching.
   C) Convey to students that only through high scholastic achievement can one become truly educated.
   D) Implement closely the opinions of adults who have already been through the educational process.
   E) Help students acquire the skills for learning.

3. It can be inferred from the passage that the educated person must

   A) Possess more maturity than passion.
   B) Not be less than forty years of age.
   C) Be at least a university graduate.
   D) Have read classic works of literature.
   E) Have traveled widely in order to understand his or her own culture.

4. Which of the following pairs of words most closely describes the author's attitude toward adults as mentioned in the passage?

A) Uninformed participants

B) Unfortunate victims

C) Conscientious citizens

D) Invaluable partners

E) Disdainful culprits

5. How is the previous passage organized?

A) An objective analysis is put forth supported by factual examples.

B) A single idea is presented with which the author does not agree.

C) A thesis is presented and support given for it.

D) Two ideas are contrasted and a conciliatory viewpoint emerges.

E) A popular viewpoint is criticized from a number of perspectives.

Appendix VII—Tips for Taking Reading Tests

Woody Allen once joked: "I took a speed reading course and read *War and Peace* in twenty minutes. It involves Russia." Well, so much for the details! This appendix is especially applicable for anyone preparing to write tests that involve reading comprehension. Reading comprehension is tested on virtually every standardized exam—including the ACT, SAT, GRE, GMAT, LSAT, and MCAT—and even appears on job placement exams. Typically, candidates are given three or four passages (each passage being two to four paragraphs in length) and asked to answer three to six multiple-choice questions per passage. The test taker is required to choose the best answer on the basis of what is stated or implied in each passage.

Strategies and Approaches

1. Read for content, noting topic, scope, and purpose.

Understanding the purpose of each passage is fundamental. As
you read a passage, keep talking silently to yourself, "What's the
purpose . . . where is the author going?" In other words, ask yourself, "Why did the author write the passage?"

*2. Read the first sentence first, then scroll down and read the last
sentence next.*

A good tip is to read the first sentence of the passage and then read
the last sentence of the passage, then start back reading at the top.
Why? Because an author (of a passage) might conclude on the last
line, and if you read this as soon as possible, you will know where
the author is going with his or her discussion, and be better able to
remember pertinent details.

*3. Read for structure, noting important "guide" words as well as the
number of viewpoints and relationship among those viewpoints.*

Keep close track of "guide" words such as "however," "but,"
"moreover," and "hence." These words are important and may
influence dramatically the flow of the passage. Next, think in
terms of the number of paragraphs and viewpoints presented.
Usually one paragraph represents one viewpoint. Frequently,
reading comprehension passages will contain two viewpoints
and it may be helpful to try and simplify everything into simple
black-and-white terms. For example, take a hypothetical passage
written about personality development. Ask yourself what is the
relationship between, say, the three paragraphs of the passage.
Perhaps the first paragraph is the introduction, the second paragraph is how sociologists view personality development, the third
paragraph is how biologists view personality development . . . now
you've got it!

4. Eliminate common wrong answer choices including out of scopes, distortions, and opposites.

There are three common wrong answer choices in reading comprehension. These include "out of scope," "opposite," and "distorted" answer choices. Note that although "irrelevant" answer choices are possible (and common wrong answer choices among critical reasoning problems), they are not common wrong answer choices in reading comprehension.

Reading Comprehension Snapshot

There is an obvious difference between the kind of casual reading that takes place when reading a newspaper and the kind required when one encounters reading comprehension in an exam format. There are essentially five areas to cover when discussing strategies to tackle reading comprehension passages and accompanying multiple-choice questions. Mastering reading comprehension involves an understanding of passage type, passage content, and passage structure, as well as passage question types and common wrong answer choices.

I. Passage Type

- ❖ Social science
- ❖ Science

II. Passage Content

- ❖ Topic
- ❖ Scope
- ❖ Purpose (equals main idea)

III. Passage Stricture

- ❖ Transition or guide words
- ❖ Number of paragraphs and their function
- ❖ Number of viewpoints and their relationships

IV. PASSAGE QUESTION TYPES

- ❖ Overview questions
- ❖ Explicit-detail questions
- ❖ Inference questions
- ❖ Tone questions
- ❖ Passage organization questions

V. COMMON WRONG ANSWER CHOICES

- ❖ Out of scope
- ❖ Opposite
- ❖ Distortion
- ❖ Irrelevant
- ❖ Too general
- ❖ Too detailed

Passage Type

There are three basic types of reading comprehension passages—social science, science, and business/economics. Since business and economics passages read more similar to social science than science, they fit easily under the umbrella of social science. The fundamental difference between social science and science is that science passages tend to be objective and generally exist to *describe*. Social science passages tend to be subjective and usually exist to *argue*. Social science (which deals with people, societies, and their institutions) is typically the domain of ideas, opinions, and conjecture while science (which deals with nature and the universe) is typically the domain of phenomena, theories, and details.

Viewpoints (ideas) and the flow of ideas (order) are generally more important in social science readings than in science readings. In terms of understanding a social science passage, it is critical to understand the author's stance—"what side the author is on." A fitting analogy is to say that social science passages are "river-rafting rides" where the goal is to not fall off our raft amid the twists and turns. Science passages are "archeological digs." Once we determine where to dig, we must keep track of the small pieces—we must be able to memorize and work with details.

Passage Content

Obviously, the better we understand what we have read, the better our chance of answering questions related to the subject at hand. In breaking down passage content, we can subdivide everything into three areas, namely topic, scope, and purpose.

Topic is defined as "the broad subject matter of the passage." Scope is defined as "the specific aspect of the topic that the author is interested in." Purpose is defined as "the author's main reason for writing the passage" or "why did the author sit down to write this passage." In short, *topic* and *scope* are "what" a passage is about while *purpose* is about "why" the passage was written.

One tip involves always performing a "topic-scope-purpose" drill. That is, always ask yourself what is the topic, scope, and purpose. Let's test this.

> The whale is the largest mammal in the animal kingdom. When most people think of whales, they think of sluggish, obese animals, frolicking freely in the ocean by day and eating tons of food to sustain themselves. When people think of ants, on the other hand, they tend to think of hardworking underfed creatures transporting objects twice their body size to and from hidden hideaways. However, if we analyze food consumption based on body size, we find that ants eat their full body weight every day while a whale eats the equivalent of only one-thousandth of its body weight each day. In fact, when we compare the proportionate food consumption of all living creatures, we find that the whale is one of the most food efficient creatures on earth.

What is the topic? The answer is clearly "whales." Don't be fooled into thinking that the topic is the "animal kingdom." This would be an example of an answer that is too general. What is the scope? The answer is "food consumption of whales." What is the purpose of the passage or why did the author sit down to write this? The author's purpose is to say that whales are food efficient creatures and to thereby counter the popular misconception that they are "biological" gas guzzlers.

Passage Structure

There are essentially two distinct ways to analyze passage structure: the micro and the macro. Micro analysis involves keeping track of transitions, which signal the flow of the passage. "Guide" words, including such words as "but" and "however," have been called the traffic lights of language. These words serve one of four primary purposes: to show continuation, illustration, contrast, or conclusion. See **Exhibit A** on the following page.

Exhibit A   Guide Words

I. Continuation Words
GREEN LIGHT

"Keep going in the same direction"

Examples:
- moreover • furthermore
- on the one hand
- undoubtedly • coincidentally

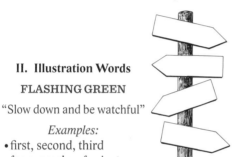

II. Illustration Words
FLASHING GREEN

"Slow down and be watchful"

Examples:
- first, second, third
- for example • for instance
- in fact • case in point

III. Contrast Words
FLASHING YELLOW

"Get ready to turn"

Examples:
- however • but • yet
- on the other hand
- whereas • conversely

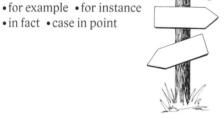

IV. Conclusion Words
RED LIGHT

"You're about to arrive"

Examples:
- in conclusion
- finally • clearly
- hence • so • thus
- therefore • as a result

Exhibit B   Passage Structure and Viewpoint

One Viewpoint

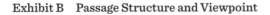

A single viewpoint is presented with which the author agrees.

Structure: [=A]

Example: "Heredity is the most important factor in personality development. Let's explore this topic."

A single viewpoint is presented with which the author does not agree.

Structure: [≠A]

Example: "Green is <u>not</u> the most versatile color. There are several reasons for this."

Two Viewpoints

Non-competing viewpoints:

Two viewpoints are presented without comparison or conflict.

Structure: [A, B]

Example: "Gold is a precious metal and diamonds are precious gems."

Complementary viewpoints:

One viewpoint builds on another viewpoint.

Structure: [A → B]

Example: "The invention of the automobile has paved the way for the invention of the airplane."

Competing viewpoints:

One of two viewpoints is deemed to be the clear winner, the other inferior.

Structure: [A>B or B>A]

Example: "Our environment is a more important factor in personality development than is heredity."

Exhibit B (*Cont'd*)

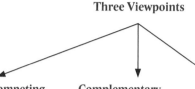

Three Viewpoints

Non-competing viewpoints:	Complementary viewpoints:	Competing viewpoints:
Three viewpoints are presented without comparison or conflict.	A third superior viewpoint is considered to be the product of two original viewpoints.	One of the three viewpoints is deemed to be the clear winner, the others inferior.
Structure: $[A, B, C]$	**Structure:** $[A + B \rightarrow C]$	**Structure:** $[C > A \text{ or } B]$
Example: "Fruits, vegetables, and proteins are part of a healthy diet."	**Example:** "The invention of the automobile and jet plane have led to the invention of the space craft."	**Example:** "Treatment C is more effective than treatment A or treatment B."

Macro analysis involves not only noting the number of paragraphs and their function, but more importantly, the number of viewpoints and their relationship. The relationships between or among viewpoints are finite and summarized in **Exhibit B**.

In terms of paragraphs and their functions, the opening paragraph is usually the introduction and each succeeding paragraph takes on a single viewpoint or concept. Passages with one or two viewpoints are most common on reading passages, although three viewpoints within a single reading comprehension passage is a possibility. As already noted, viewpoints are more applicable to social science passages than to science passages because social science is typically subjective and argumentative.

Passage Question Types

There are five basic kinds of reading comprehension questions.
These include: (1) overview questions, (2) explicit-detail questions,
(3) inference questions, (4) tone questions, and (5) passage organization questions. Examples of each question type follow.

Overview questions

"The primary purpose of this passage is to . . ." or "Which of the following is the author's main idea?" Not surprisingly, an overview question
is sometimes called a primary purpose or main idea question.

Explicit-detail questions

"According to the passage, the author states that . . ." An explicit-detail
question is a question which has a very literal answer. It is something
that the reader has read and it can be confirmed based on words actually written in the passage.

Inference questions

"It can be inferred from the passage that . . ." or "The author implies
that . . ." The artistry in answering an inference question lies in drawing that magic line between what can be logically inferred based on
information in a passage and what is declared outside the scope of
the passage.

Tone questions

"The attitude of the author toward mystics can best be described as . . ."
A tone question asks the reader to comment on the "temperature" of
some aspect of the passage.

Passage organization questions

"Which of the following best describes the way in which this passage is
organized?" A passage organization question asks about the structure
of the passage or the structure of a portion of the passage.

Exhibit C The Four-Corner Question Cracker for Reading Comprehension™

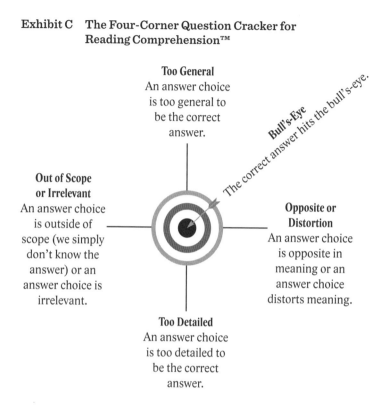

Too General
An answer choice is too general to be the correct answer.

Bull's-Eye
The correct answer hits the bull's-eye.

Out of Scope or Irrelevant
An answer choice is outside of scope (we simply don't know the answer) or an answer choice is irrelevant.

Opposite or Distortion
An answer choice is opposite in meaning or an answer choice distorts meaning.

Too Detailed
An answer choice is too detailed to be the correct answer.

The four-quadrant grid above, per **Exhibit C**, is a useful tool to ferret out common wrong answer choices on reading comprehension questions. The correct answer always appears in the middle where the bull's-eye is located. The four incorrect answers will almost always appear in one of the four corners.

Common Wrong Answer Choices

Out of Scope: An out of scope answer choice is an answer choice that cannot be answered based on information in the passage. An out of scope statement may, in fact, be right or wrong, but it is not something that can be determined based on information supplied by the passage.

Irrelevant: An irrelevant answer choice is an answer choice that in no way touches the topic; it is completely off target. We might contrast irrelevant answer choices with out of scope answer choices in that an out of scope answer choice is related tangentially to the passage, whereas the irrelevant answer choice is not. Think of an archer with bow and arrow. Out of scope means that the archer is missing the target, but at least he or she is shooting at the right target, and in the right direction. Irrelevant means that the archer isn't even shooting at the correct target.

Opposite: An opposite answer choice is an answer choice which is opposite in meaning to a statement or viewpoint expressed or implied by the passage. One common way answer choices are used to reverse meaning is through the inclusion or omission of prefixes such as "in," "un," and "dis," or the inclusion or omission of negative words such as "no" or "not." Thus "unfortunately" becomes "fortunately," "advantageous" becomes "disadvantageous," and "not applicable" becomes "applicable."

Distortion: A distorted answer choice is an answer choice that distorts the meaning of something stated or implied by the passage. Saying, for example, that something is "good" is not the same as saying that something is "best." Distortions are typically signaled by the use of extreme wording or by the use of categorical words such as "any," "all," "always," "cannot," "never," "only," and "solely."

Too General: This answer choice is relevant only to the overview question type. Examples: A discussion of "South American trade imbalances in the 1950s" is not the same thing as a discussion of "modern global economic practices." The latter is obviously broader in scope: "global" is broader than "South American"; "modern" is broader than "the 1950s"; "economics" encompasses more than just "trade imbalances."

Too Detailed: This answer choice is also relevant only to overview-type questions. Example: A discussion of "the propagation of the Venus Fly Trap" is a much more specific topic than is "plant reproductive systems." The correct answer to an overview-type question is, relative to the topic, neither overly general nor overly detailed.

Let's gain further insight into how test makers may create incorrect answer choices with respect to reading comprehension (as well as critical reasoning) questions. Take the following easy-to-understand statement:

> **Original:** "Success is a strange phenomenon. You can achieve it through hard work, skill, or luck, or some combination of the three."

Here are several concocted statements derived from the original statement which showcase incorrect answer choices.

Out of scope:
"The *most* important ingredient in success is hard work."
> (COMMENT: No, we don't know whether hard work is the most important element in achieving success.)

"Hard work is a *more* important element in success than is skill."
> (COMMENT: Unwarranted comparison—we don't know which element, in relative terms, is more important than the other.)

Irrelevant:
"People who achieve success through hard work, skill, or luck sometimes find that their lives are meaningless."
> (COMMENT: We are only concerned with how to achieve success, not what might happen beyond that juncture.)

Opposite:
"People who are either hardworking, skillful, or lucky are *not* likely to achieve success."
> (COMMENT: The word "not" reverses the meaning of the original statement.)

Distortion:

"*Only* through hard work can one achieve success."
> (COMMENT: No, we can also achieve success by being skillful or lucky. The word "only" creates a distortion.)

"A person who is hardworking does not run *any* risk of failure."
> (COMMENT: The word "any" distorts the meaning of the original statement. How likely is the possibility of engaging in any human endeavor and having no chance of failure. This statement may also be viewed as out of scope because the original statement makes no mention of the word "failure.")

"A person who is hardworking, skillful, or lucky can achieve *greatness*."
> (COMMENT: The word "greatness" has an elevated meaning as compared with "success." Another way to view this statement is that it is out of scope because the original statement does not make mention of what it takes to achieve greatness.)

The Relationship Between Question Types and Common Wrong Answer Choices

How might the different reading comprehension question types be tackled based on an understanding of the common wrong answer choices?

(1) Overview questions

There are at least four ways to avoid wrong answer choices when tackling overview questions.

i) Consider eliminating any answer choice which does not contain the words of the topic. Note that this advice works well for Q1, page 184.

ii) Avoid any *overly detailed* answer choice which may be a factually correct statement, but which is too detailed to be the correct answer choice to an overview question.

iii) Avoid any *overly general* answer choice that is too broad to represent the topic at hand.

iv) Use a verb scan, when possible. That is, look at the verb which begins each answer choice and eliminate those verbs which do not fit. Five common verbs found in reading comprehension passages include *describe*, *discuss*, *explain*, *argue*, and *criticize*. "Argue" is found frequently in social science passages; "describe" is found frequently in science passages. "Discuss" and "explain" are found in both social science and science passages. "Criticize" is usually not correct in an overview question involving a science passage because the author is typically out to describe something without being opinionated or judgmental.

(2) Explicit-detail questions and (3) Inference questions

On both explicit-detail questions and inference questions, common wrong answer choices include *opposites* and *out of scopes*.

Inference questions are especially vulnerable to wrong answer choices that are beyond the scope of the passage. In the context of a standardized test question, the test taker must be careful not to assume too much. Standardized test questions are notorious for narrowing the scope of what we can infer based on what we read. Contrast this with everyday life in which we generally use a loose framework and assume a lot.

(4) Tone questions

Tone is attitude and there are basically three "temperatures" for tone questions—positive, negative, or neutral. One trick is to avoid answer choices which contain "verbally confused word pairs." For example, the word pairs "supercilious disdain" or "self-mingled pity" are not terribly clear. Test makers like to include these types of answer choices believing that test takers will be attracted to confusing, complex sounding wrong answer choices.

(5) Passage organization questions

Two classic structures arise in reading comprehension passages. The first relates to social science passages, where a common structure is "A > B." Given that the hallmark of social science passages is their provocative, subjective, and often argumentative nature, such passages often contain competing viewpoints, where one view is favored over another. The other classic structure relates to science passages, which are often structured in the form of "A, B." An important distinction with regard to the latter is that the two events are simply being described in detail, but not contrasted. Because science passages exist classically to describe (not to criticize), the author is unlikely to show favoritism to one side.

Regardless of the structure of the passage, a reader should always be careful to distinguish between the author's view and that of the information and evidence in the passage itself. For instance, the author may present information that clearly favors one side of an issue, especially if there is more support for that side or the stance is compelling. However, he or she may not necessarily endorse that viewpoint. Remember that "what the passage says" and "what the author thinks" may not always be one in the same. For example, an author of a passage may present evidence as to why the scientific community, in general, is skeptical about a belief in psychics, but that doesn't necessarily mean that the author is skeptical about a belief in psychics.

Note: Two caveats that must be noted when using the *The Four-Corner Question Cracker for Reading Comprehension*™. The first is that it can only be used on three of the five question types, namely *overview* questions, *explicit-detail* questions, and *inference* questions. That said, this is hardly problematic because these three question types are by far the most common question types found in reading comprehension. In fact, they may even be referred to as the "big 3" question types for reading comprehension. Second, the vertical grid of the four-corner question cracker, which highlights *too general* answer choices and *too detailed* answer choices, can only be used when tackling *overview* questions. That is, the vertical grid cannot be used on *explicit-detail* or *inference* questions. In short, wrong answer choices on *explicit-detail* and *inference* questions are strictly referred to as being out of scope, opposite in meaning, or distorted in meaning.

Answers and Explanations

Note that some problems have definitive solutions. For others, where there is no single "right" answer, a proposed solution is provided.

Chapter 2: Creative Thinking

PROBLEM 1   ONE STROKE

Oh, how easy it is to be trapped by a programmed mindset and conclude, "There's no answer here!"

$$SIX = 6$$

Another solution is:

$$IX \neq 6$$

Here's another solution (although the instructions don't actually say you can reposition a character):

$$IX = 9$$

PROBLEM 2   MOP

The floor is dirty because Sally used a dirty mop, and before she used the mop the floor was clean!

PROBLEM 3   PATTERN

There are two possible solutions to this problem. The first solution below could be accurate if the pattern alternates with one on top and three on the bottom. This solution is also accurate if we put vowels on the top and consonants on the bottom.

A second solution is possible if we put letters consisting only of straight lines on top and letters consisting of curves on the bottom.

Problem 4 Nine Dots

The "Nine Dots Game" serves as an example of a self-imposed barrier to creativity. As can be seen in the first solution below, the lines can be drawn outside of the perimeter formed by the nine dots. This usually cannot be seen because we are programmed to keep the lines within the boxed area. Another possibility, as depicted by the solution on the right, occurs by drawing lines that touch the corners of the various dots. Nothing states that the lines have to be drawn through the centers of the dots.

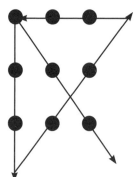

Problem 5 Two Water Buckets

1. Fill the 5-gallon bucket

2. Pour 5-gallon bucket into 3-gallon bucket

3. Dump water from the 3-gallon bucket

4. Pour the 2 gallons contained in the 5-gallon bucket into the 3-gallon bucket

5. Refill the 5-gallon bucket (5 gallons + 2 gallons = 7 gallons)

Chapter 3: Decision Making

PROBLEM 6   CORPORATE TRAINING

Pros	Cons
Yes, I agree that we should provide in-house training.	No, I dont think we should provide in-house training.

Quantitative Support Points

Pros	Cons
• Increased revenue—builds skilled employees who are more productive.	• Decreased cost—saves money as a result of bypassing training costs.
• Decreased cost—cuts down on costs of hiring from outside the company.	• Increased revenue—company may be able to hire trained employees from existing job pool or from another company.
• Increased revenue—training can be tailored to specific company needs for immediate benefit.	• Decreased cost—investments (benefits) are lost due to the high rate of employee turnover.

Qualitative Support Points

Pros	Cons
• Increases employee morale.	• Saves time.
• Builds loyalty of employees to company.	• Employees may prefer cash bonuses in lieu of training courses.
• Builds the company's image; organization will be perceived as a leader by virtue of its confidence in implementing in-house training programs.	• Avoiding training may keep the company from being forced to continue or expand training, as instituting training programs creates a precedent to continue such programs in the future.

PROBLEM 7   SINGLES

Answer: 66⅔%. Two-thirds of the women are single (i.e., $^{20}/_{30} = ^2/_3$).
A truly easy way to do this problem is to assume for simplicity's sake
that there are 100 students in the course and fill in the given information, turning percentages into numbers. For example, if 70 percent
of the students are male, then 30 percent must be female. If we assume
there are 100 students then 70 are male and 30 are female. With this
method, visualize the percentages in the matrixes below as being actual
numbers and appearing without percent signs.

First, plug the given data from the problem into the matrix:

	Male	Female	
Married	20%		30%
Single		?	
	70%	?	

Second, complete the matrix, totaling down and across:

	Male	Female	
Married	20%	10%	30%
Single	50%	20%	70%
	70%	30%	100%

Problem 8   Batteries

Answer: 4%. To obtain the percentage of defective batteries sold by the factory, we fill in the information per the following matrix to obtain $3/75$ or $1/25$ or 4%. Picking the number "100" (which assumes 100 is the total number of batteries) greatly simplifies the task at hand.

First, plug the given data from the problem into the matrix:

	Defective	Not Defective	
Rejected		$1/10\,(80) = 8$	$1/4\,(100) = 25$
Not Rejected	?		?
	$1/5\,(100) = 20$	80	100

Second, complete the matrix, totaling down and across:

	Defective	Not Defective	
Rejected	17	8	25
Not Rejected	3	72	75
	20	80	100

Problem 9   Interrogation

Answer: 7%. Seven percent of all subjects will end up confessing to the crime and rightfully so—"They're admitting they did it and they really did do it!"

Step 1: Fill in the given information.

	Subject committed the crime	Subject did not commit the crime	
Subject is telling the truth	?		
Subject is not telling the truth		2%	20%
		75%	

Step 2: Complete the matrix, totaling down and across:

	Subject committed the crime	Subject did not commit the crime	
Subject is telling the truth	7%	73%	80%
Subject is not telling the truth	18%	2%	20%
	25%	75%	100%

PROBLEM 10 SET MENU

Answer: 24. The diagram that follows serves both as a decision-event tree and a probability tree. First, there are twenty-four ways by which a diner can choose his or her meal. Second, if we assume that every

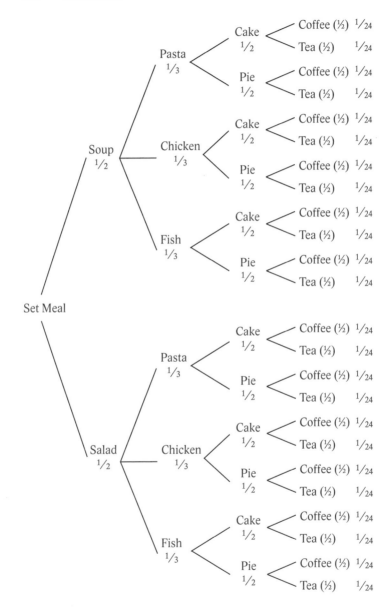

dish has an equal probability of being chosen, then the probability of any meal being chosen is $1/24$. For example, one person could choose soup, pasta, pie, and coffee ($1/2 \times 1/3 \times 1/2 \times 1/2 = /24$). Another person might choose salad, fish, cake, and tea ($1/2 \times 1/3 \times 1/2 \times 1/2 = 1/24$).

PROBLEM 11 INVESTOR
Answer: $55,000.

First Investment:

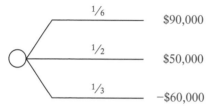

Second Investment:

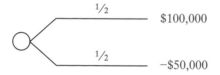

Third Investment:

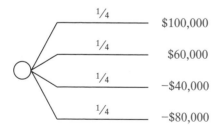

First Investment:
WA = $90K(1/6) + $50K(1/2) + –$60K(1/3) = $20K

Second Investment:
WA = $100K(1/2) + –$50K(1/2) = $25K

Third Investment:
WA = $100K(1/4) = $60K(1/4) + –$40K(1/4) + –$80K(1/4) = $10K

So, the aggregate value of all three investments is:
Expected Return = $20,000 + $25,000 + $10,000 = $55,000

Note: Expected Return is calculated using the weighted average formula.

Chapter 4: Analyzing Arguments

Comparison and Analogy Assumptions:

PROBLEM 12   CRIME

Choice E. The key to understanding this problem is to recognize the scope shift that occurs as a result of switching terms from "crime" to "reported crime." Obviously, reported crime is not the same thing as actual crime. As answer choice E states: "It is possible for reported crime to have gone down while actual crime has remained the same or actually gone up." In order to make comparisons we need to stick to terms that are of equivalent meaning.

Choice A is incorrect. This answer choice slightly strengthens, not weakens, the original argument. In choice B, it does not matter whether police officers, as citizens themselves, voted for a bill on initiatives to reduce crime in the city. It also does not matter, as in choice C, whether most arrests were repeat offenders. Whether first-time offenders or repeat offenders, crime is crime.

The fact that crime has come to include white-collar crime (choice D) actually strengthens the argument. It suggests that there could be more incidences of crime (or cases of reported crime), which makes a decrease in crime (or cases of reported crime) potentially that much more significant.

PROBLEM 13   HYPERACTIVITY

Choice D. The idea that more types of behavior are deemed hyperactive indeed weakens the claim that children today are more hyperactive than they were ten years ago. In short, there are more ways to "check off" and confirm hyperactive behavior. In order to compare the hyperactivity of children today versus ten years ago, we need an even playing field in terms of the comparability of terms— the definition of hyperactivity or the criteria for hyperactive behavior must remain consistent over time. Choices A and B are effectively out of the argument's scope. We are not talking about creativity and spontaneity, nor are we primarily concerned about other potentially more serious issues beyond hyperactivity. The impact of having more or fewer pictures in children's books remains unclear (choice C) as does an increase in ailments such as Attention Deficit Hyperactivity Disorder (ADHD) per choice E.

Representativeness Assumptions:

PROBLEM 14   MOVIE BUFFS

Choice B. This is a classic representative sample assumption question. The argument assumes that a sample based on people attending Sunday matinees (afternoon showings) is representative of the whole country of moviegoers. The question is, "How representative is the opinion of those attending Sunday matinees?" For example, Sunday matinee moviegoers might consist of a disproportionate number of family viewers (i.e., people with children) who prefer not to watch bizarre or violent movies during their Sunday afternoons. For this sample to be representative, we need to survey at least some Saturday night moviegoers, Saturday matinee moviegoers, and weekday moviegoers.

Choice A does weaken the argument somewhat by suggesting that people will see a movie regardless of its genre just so long as their star actor (or actress) appears. Choice C is incorrect because we are concerned about the current tastes of moviegoers and not the movie hits of yesteryear.

Choice D is incorrect. We cannot assume that increased book sales and college enrollment in criminology courses is necessarily linked to trends among moviegoers. As far as we know, the moderate increase in course enrollments is the result of many other factors.

Choice E is incorrect because it notionally strengthens the idea that movie producers should stop producing these types of movies because they are financially unsound. If actors' salaries are high, then movie production costs will be higher, putting pressure on the bottom line.

Problem 15   Bull Market

Choice A. This argument assumes that the whole of the Indian economy can be judged from the strength of the stock market, here the National Stock Exchange (NSE) index. In choice B, the fact that the Bombay Stock Exchange (BSE) index (another major stock exchange in India) has gone up does lend support for the comments made, but it does not lend as much support as does choice A. Choice A provides direct support for the key assumption in the argument.

The fact that the National Stock Exchange (NSE) index was down this time last year, choice C, neither lends support for nor weakens the argument at hand. The fact that the Asian and European economies are also considered strong (choice D) lends some tangential support to a strong Indian economy, but it is hard to draw any firm conclusions from this fact. The fact that the National Stock Exchange (NSE) index is subject to great fluctuations (choice E) serves to weaken the comments made.

This is essentially the same argument used in the example titled "Finland" in *Chapter 2*, which may also be viewed under the guise of a representativeness assumption. The argument concludes (in the "general") that Finland is the most technologically advanced country on earth; the argument uses as evidence (in the "particular") the fact that more people per capita own mobile phones in Finland than anywhere else on earth.

Problem 16   Putting

Choice C. The argument assumes that the ability to putt is the pivotal factor in determining whether a person can achieve a low golf score. A good golf game has many ingredients, including putting, driving, iron shots, chipping, sand trap shots, judging weather, pacing, strategy, temperament, experience, physical fitness, and competitiveness. This passage assumes that it all happens on the putting green. Although it would be impossible to argue that putting is not an important component to achieving a low score in golf, it is certainly not the only factor.

Choice A is incorrect. We cannot assume that there is no way to improve a golf game other than with quality equipment. Practice itself might be enough to improve a golf game. The argument does suggest that if a person wants to make great improvements in his or her golf game then he or she needs to make improvements in putting and, ideally, purchase a new Sweet Spot Putter.

Choice B is incorrect because it forms an unwarranted comparison that is not assumed in the argument. We do not know whether a new Sweet Spot Putter will improve an amateur's game more than it will improve a professional's game or vice-versa. Likewise, choice D is incorrect because we do not know whether the new Sweet Spot Putter is superior to any other putter currently on the market. For all we know, the Sweet Spot Putter is just one of three new miracle putters.

Per choice E, we also have no way of knowing whether lessons are, or are not, as effective at improving the accuracy of a player's putting as is the use of quality equipment.

Note: Broadly speaking, representativeness assumptions are applicable any time that we argue from the particular to the general. Surveys or questionnaires are often used as the basis for representative sample assumptions, as seen in problem 14, titled *Movie Buffs*. In problem 15, titled *Bull Market*, the strength of the Indian economy (the "general") is based on the strength of the National Stock Exchange (NSE) index (the "particular"). In the problem at hand, success in the game of golf is assumed to rest primarily on the ability to make putts. Here again, we argue primarily from the particular ("putting") to the general ("golf").

"Good Evidence" Assumptions:

PROBLEM 17   CRITIC'S CHOICE
Choice C. Since there are certainly far more than 100 contemporary and 100 non-contemporary novels to choose from, a question arises as to whether those novels chosen are representative of the entire population of contemporary and non-contemporary novels. It is possible that the author of *Decline of the Novelist* chose novels which best supported his/her thesis—that today's novelists are not as skillful as the novelists of yesteryear. Choice A might weaken the argument slightly but certainly wouldn't weaken it seriously. Choice B, while highly plausible, is irrelevant to the argument because the author focuses his/her argument on technical skill. Choice D is simply out of scope since we don't know anything about the literary skill required to do screenplays. Choice E is irrelevant; it doesn't matter whether the average reader is familiar with the terms of literary criticism; it only matters that the book's author is familiar with these terms.

PROBLEM 18   TEMPERAMENT
Choice E. This is an example of proof by selected instances. Each person—Steve and John—will simply choose examples which support his intended claim. Steve picks red-haired people who have bad tempers to support his claim that red-haired people are bad tempered. John picks red-haired people who have good tempers to support his claim that red-haired people are not bad-tempered. The fact that the number

of red-haired people (choice A) that one person knows is more or less than the number of red-haired people that the other person knows has no clear effect on reconciling the two statements. In fact, it is quite possible that the percentage of red-haired people that each knows is quite close, say 5 percent. After all, that's the magic of percentages as opposed to numbers—percentages express things in relative terms. In choice B, it is only plausible that the number of red-haired people both Steve and John know would be, in aggregate, less than the total of non-red-haired people that both know. Confirmation of this likely reality will not reconcile the two seemingly contradictory statements.

It is also unclear whether choice C has any effect. Any mis-assessments may prove net positive or net negative or may have a counterbalancing effect. It is almost axiomatic that both Steve and John know of friends who are not red-haired and have bad tempers, but this will do nothing to reconcile the contradictory statements, so choice D is out. Note that the procedure for actually proving whether or not red hair is correlated with bad temper falls within the context of experimental design. Refer to Hypothesis Testing in *Chapter 3*.

Note: Here is a follow-up problem which mimics a true-to-life scenario. Surveys or questionnaires completed and returned may not be representative of respondents' viewpoints in general if surveys or questionnaires not returned would have yielded conflicting information.

PRESIDENT: I'm worried about the recent turnover in MegaCorp. If employees leave our company disgruntled, such negative feelings can hurt our reputation in the marketplace.

HUMAN RESOURCES MANAGER: Your concerns are unfounded. As part of our post-employment follow-up process, we send questionnaires to each employee within thirty days of his or her leaving the company. These questionnaires seek honest answers and remind employees that all responses will be kept confidential. Of the last 100 employees who left our company, 25 have responded, and only 5 people have mentioned having had any negative employment experience.

The Human Resource Manager's argument is most vulnerable to criticism on the grounds that it fails to acknowledge the possibility that

A)   Opinions expressed in such questionnaires are not always indicative of how employees actually felt.

B)   Many of those who harbored truly negative feelings about their employment experience at MegaCorp did not respond to the questionnaire.

C)   The Public Relations firm Quantum, recently hired by MegaCorp has successfully designed several programs specially aimed at boosting the company's public image.

D)   Questions asking about negative employment experiences have been placed at the end, not at the beginning, of the questionnaire.

E)   The response rate in general for questionnaires is 10 percent, meaning that only 1 in 10 questionnaires can be expected to be completed and returned.

The correct answer is choice B. If those former employees of MegaCorp who harbor very negative feeling about the company remain silent (i.e., they don't respond to the questionnaire), then such views have been omitted from inclusion. Choice A may also be a concern, but it is impossible to tell whether it refers to employees who felt much better about their employment experience or much worse (we can't assume employees necessarily felt worse!). In choice C, we can't assume that the public relations efforts of Quantum have any affect on the employees who have left the company; besides, designing and implementing programs are two different things. The placement of questions within the questionnaire (choice D) is likely irrelevant or its impact inconclusive. Choice E strengthens the Human Resource Manager's claim because the response rate achieved by MegaCorp (i.e., $^{25}/_{100} = 25\%$)

is greater than the general response rate of 10 percent; of course, the higher the response rate the better.

Cause-and-Effect Assumptions:

PROBLEM 19   CYCLIST

Choice C. This argument turns correlation into causation. There is likely a high correlation between low body fat and being a world-class cyclist. But there may well be a high correlation among other variables as well. For example, a high correlation also likely exists between muscular strength and world-class cycling, and technical skills (maneuvering a bike) and world-class cycling.

This problem can also be solved as an, "if . . . then" type problem. The original reads, "If one is a world-class cyclist, then one has 4 to 11 percent body fat." When the "if . . . then" statement is erroneously reversed and the argument becomes, "If one has 4 to 11 percent body fat, then one can be a world-class cyclist." Having low body fat is a necessary but not a sufficient condition for being a world-class cyclist. "If . . . then"–type statements are discussed in *Chapter 5*.

PROBLEM 20   SAT SCORES

Choice B. The argument basically says that SAT scores have gone up because students are better test takers, not because students possess better academic skills. Are students smarter or just better test takers?

Choices A and E may appear tricky. Actually the author doesn't deny his opponents' figures or suggest his evidence is flawed. In fact, the author agrees with his opponents' facts (test scores are getting higher). What the author is saying is that his opponents' evidence is incomplete, not flawed. Choice D is not correct. The argument is not flawed due to circular reasoning. In circular reasoning, a conclusion is based on evidence, and that same piece of evidence is based on the conclusion. Choice D in this problem is incorrect for the same reason that choice E is incorrect in the previous problem, *Cyclist*. An argument that assumes what it seeks to establish is a circular argument.

Cause-and-effect fallacies exist when there is confusion about the causal relationship between two events. See if the argument is set up in terms of some situation "A" causing some situation "B." Ask, "Is A really causing event B?" Show that A does not necessarily lead to B, and the argument is weakened or falls apart.

Here is a summary of how both arguments unfold:

OPPONENT'S ARGUMENT:

Conclusion: Students are better skilled.

Evidence: Parents are impressed.

Evidence: Test scores are getting higher.

Assumption: There is a strong correlation between higher test scores and better skills. That is, parents are impressed because higher scores are an indication that students are better skilled.

AUTHOR'S ARGUMENT:

Conclusion: Students are better test takers, not better skilled academically.

Evidence: Studies confirm students are weaker in the basics.

Evidence: Test scores are getting higher.

Assumption: There exists no strong correlation between higher test scores and better skills.

Note: *SAT* is a problem that serves to highlight the importance of identifying the evidence and conclusion, as well as the underlying assumption which links the evidence with the conclusion. In advancing another example, consider the person who says, "No wonder Todd chose to attend a good university; he was setting himself up for the good job after graduation." We cannot assume that Todd went to university for the purpose of getting a good job afterward. He may have gone to university to play on a varsity sports team, with the hope of playing professional sports. He may have gone purely for the academic experience, with no vocational thoughts at all, and then again, he may have gone just to get away from home, meet new friends, and enjoy himself socially.

Let's explore further the topic of alternative causal explanations. Focus on each argument's assumption.

AUTHOR'S ORIGINAL ARGUMENT:

Conclusion: The reason Todd chose to go to a good university was to get a good job upon graduation.

Evidence: Todd went to a good university. He got a good job upon graduation.

Assumption: Going to a good university caused Todd to get a good job upon graduation.

Argument #1: The sports person

Conclusion: Todd went to a good university for the purpose of playing on a nationally recognized varsity sports team.

Evidence: Todd went to a good university. He played on a nationally recognized varsity sports team.

Assumption: A person would not go to a good university and play on a well-known varsity sports team unless that was his or her primary motivation for doing so.

Argument #2: The academic

Conclusion: Todd went to university for the academic challenge.

Evidence: Todd went to a good university. He excelled academically.

Assumption: A person would not go to university and excel academically unless that was his or her primary objective for going to university.

Argument #3: The socialite

Conclusion: Todd went to a good university to improve himself socially.

Evidence: Todd went to a good university. He joined several well-known clubs on campus and met many new friends.

Assumption: A person would not go to university and join several well-known clubs unless motivated to do so for social reasons.

PROBLEM 21 VALDEZ

Choice E. This choice would most weaken the original argument. Making a plausible alternative explanation serves to undermine the idea that Ms. Valdez's international marketing program was the reason for the jump in profits from 8–15 percent. The alternative explanation suggests that the increase in profits is due to a corporate acquisition prior to Ms. Valdez's appointment as president which doubled Zipco's annual revenues. We do have to assume in choice E that revenues and profits are linked proportionately; nonetheless it is still the best choice.

None of choices A through D bring us close enough to increased revenues or profits. They all mention potentially positive things, but we don't have a clear assurance that they brought in the bucks (dollars). Choice B, perhaps the best wrong answer choice, simply says that production capacity has increased. We do not know whether an increase in production capacity equals an actual increase in production, or if such an increase in production has resulted in more profits.

PROBLEM 22 HEADLINE

Choice C. The idea that low self-esteem may be the cause of both obesity and depression most weakens this argument. Here, obesity and depression are deemed the joint effects of another single cause—low self-esteem.

Per choice A, it is not essential to the argument that one understands why he or she is depressed or how to escape from depression's grip. It is only essential that obesity be the cause of depression.

In choice B, it is not necessary for obesity to be the only cause of depression; there could be many ways to become depressed besides becoming obese. In choice D, it is not necessary that obesity and depression be linked proportionally, even if causally related. Depression could occur whenever one is declared "overweight," even though it would be logical to assume that one who is more overweight is also to some degree more depressed. Per choice E, the terms "desperation" and "suicide," even if linked to depression, are outside the scope of the claim—"obesity is linked to depression."

PROBLEM 23   TV VIEWING

Choice E. One way to destroy or seriously damage a causal relationship (e.g., A causes B) is to show that it is not A that causes B but B that causes A. This is what choice E does by suggesting reverse causation. It suggests that aggressive people go looking for violent TV programming, not that violent TV programming makes people aggressive.

Choice A may weaken things a bit, but not drastically. The fact that some viewers in the high-viewing group experienced lower aggression levels than did other subjects in the high-viewing group is not an improbable result. What matters is that more high-viewers experienced more aggression overall relative to low-viewers. Ditto for choice B. Choice C is incorrect because it is irrelevant whether fear did or did not cause some viewers to restrict their viewing. If it did, it will only mean that these viewers should have shown fewer signs of aggression because they weren't viewing as much. The reason that they are not viewing is effectively irrelevant. Choice D is also irrelevant; what matters is that people actually viewed the programs, not whether the programs were live or pre-recorded.

PROBLEM 24   SHARK

Choice B. First, let's go to the incorrect answer choices. Answer A is the closest to the correct answer because it generally supports the idea that surfers in other areas are also not being attacked. Choice A slightly strengthens the original argument. Choice C weakens the argument, suggesting that there are no sharks left in the reserve. Choice D also weakens the argument by suggesting that an alternative explanation (e.g., wristbands with metal bells) may be key to understanding why sharks are not attacking surfers. Choice E is essentially irrelevant; we are talking about surfers, not divers or tuna.

In choice B (correct answer), what we really want to know is whether sharks attack surfers wearing black suits while avoiding surfers wearing metallic suits. What do you need in order to prove that metallic suits really work? The framework for setting this problem up is the basis for experimental design problems, as seen in real-life research.

	Shark attacks	No shark attacks	Total number of surfers
Black suits	(a)	(b)	xx
Metallic suits	(c)	(d)	xx
	xx	xx	xxx

This problem highlights the trap of proof by selected instances. People trying to prove the efficacy of wearing metallic suits cite examples from categories (a) and (d). That is, they cite instances of surfers wearing black suits and getting attacked by sharks (see "a") and also cite instances of surfers in metallic wet suits who do not get attacked by sharks (see "d"). People trying to prove the efficacy of wearing traditional black suits cite examples from categories (b) and (c). That is, they cite instances of surfers wearing metallic suits and getting attacked by sharks (see "c") while citing instances of surfers wearing black suits and not getting attacked by sharks (see "b").

It is quite possible that in recent months there haven't been any shark attacks. In such an event, any comparison about the efficacy of wearing metallic suits would prove fruitless, as depicted in the chart below containing hypothetical numbers.

	Shark attacks	No shark attacks	Total number of surfers
Black suits	0	950	950
Metallic suits	0	50	50
	0	1,000	1,000

If we had actual numbers for all boxes, we could make a percentage comparison to determine whether wearing a metallic suit really made a difference. The number of surfers wearing black suits who were attacked by sharks would be divided by the total number of surfers wearing black suits. The number of surfers wearing metallic suits who were attacked by sharks would be divided by the total number of surfers wearing metallic suits. A comparison of these two percentage figures would yield a conclusion.

Note: Below is an original statement enclosed in quotation marks. Which of the two statements that follow add the most support for the original statement?

Original: "Firm ABC is spending money on advertising and seeing an increase in sales. Clearly advertising is causing the increase in sales."

Statement I: Other competing firms are also spending money on advertising and seeing an increase in their sales.

Statement II: Without spending money on advertising, Firm ABC would not have seen an increase in sales.

The answer is statement II. Although statement I lends some support to the proposition that advertising expenditure is leading to an increase in the sales of Firm ABC, what we really want to know is the opposite—what happens when we do not spend money on advertising. If we do not spend money on advertising, we would expect to see a resulting decrease in current sales levels. If not, then this would call into question whether advertising is really causing our sales to increase and suggest that another cause is responsible for the increase in sales.

Implementation Assumptions:

PROBLEM 25 SOLAR ENERGY
Choice C. If research has not yet developed an effective way to capture and store solar energy in a way that most families can employ, then this would seriously weaken the argument. This "plan" will not work if we lack the prerequisite technological capability to implement the solution.

Choice A is irrelevant. Choice B slightly weakens the argument by suggesting that powerful utility monopolies are acting in their own self-interest by not presenting fair and impartial information. Choices D and E bring the issue of cost into play but the argument made suggests other considerations besides costs that favor the adoption of solar energy. For example, solar energy is superior because it eliminates air and water pollution, and in the case of nuclear energy, the threat of radiation.

PROBLEM 26 CLASSICS
Choice E. In order for a plan to work, desire or motivation on the part of the individual or organization must be present. Here, the operative word is "can" and the ability to do something does not necessarily translate to the "will" to do something. "Can" does not equal "will"!

Perhaps the easiest way to summarize the problem is to say that just because most literate people have not read the classics does not mean that they are necessarily lazy. Most literate people may simply choose not to spend their time doing so. Also, even if a person is lazy, he or she may still be able to read the classics. For example, the literate but lazy person may just read very slowly or in fits and starts but still arrive at the finish line. All we do know is that some people have likely read the classics. For all we know, some of these people might be motivated and some might be lazy. We cannot assume that all of the people who have read the classics belong to the motivated group.

Choice D is not correct because the original statement is not a true "if . . . then" statement, meaning that the contrapositive is not a valid inference, as it would otherwise be (see **Exhibit 5.3**). The original statement only states that a person who is literate and not lazy "can" read the classics.

Here is an example which illustrates how choice D might have been a correct choice. Say the original statement was a true "if . . . then" statement as follows:

Hypothetical: "If a person is literate and is not lazy then he or she <u>will</u> read the classics."

Here, the contrapositive leads to a correct inference.

Statement: "If a person has not read the classics then he or she is a literate person who is lazy!"

Note: Here is a follow-up problem highlighting a common assumption as found in an everyday setting. A plan may not be feasible due to lack of financial wherewithal.

> Economic recessions are opportunities for industrial
> change. Industries are forced to close their doors and throw
> workers out of jobs. In due course, some of the workers thus
> displaced from work become the entrepreneurs who drive

new industries; others learn new skills so that when the
economy revives they can join in a new pattern of industry.

The speaker in the passage above assumes which of the following?

A) The innovative ideas of entrepreneurs seem so radical that
they are ignored until such time as no other solutions
present themselves.

B) Economic recessions require a society to reevaluate its
economic priorities and its methods of production.

C) Some of the workers displaced by an economic recession
have, or are able to find, the financial resources to support
themselves while learning new skills.

D) The overall effect of an economic recession is to eliminate
inefficient industrial methods and thereby make room for
new industrial methods.

E) An economic recession affects all members of a society
regardless of their economic positions.

The correct answer is choice C. The original argument sounds
persuasive enough: economic recessions provide new opportunities
for persons out of work to learn new skills and again become produc-
tive. However, the passage assumes that a person has the wherewithal
(financial resources) not only to support him- or herself while out of a
job but also to pay to acquire new skills. Choices A and E are essentially
irrelevant. Choices B and D are trickier. However, these two choices
essentially restate the claim made in the original argument and do little
to damage the assumption.

Try approaching this problem using classic argument structure. The
conclusion is the very first sentence—"Economic recessions are opportunities for industrial change." The rest of the sentences are evidence,
i.e., "Industries that are forced to close throw workers out of jobs. In due
course, some of the workers thus displaced from work become the entrepreneurs who find new industries; others learn new skills so that when

the economy revives they can join in a new pattern of industry." After you re-read the conclusion, stop and ask yourself: Why are economic recessions opportunities for industrial change? The reason is contained in the evidence (or premises). Basically, they are opportunities because people can retrain themselves. Once you have answered this question, it becomes much more obvious that this argument assumes that people have the time and money to retrain themselves.

Problem 27   Public Transportation

Choice A. The fact that there may be better or easier ways to lower pollution levels in most major cities falls outside the scope of this argument. The argument only concerns itself with the idea that people should leave their cars at home and take public transportation to combat pollution. Also outside the scope of this argument would be the idea that most major cities have other more pressing problems, such as poverty, crime, or affordable housing.

This question was chosen to highlight implementation assumptions that can occur in critical reasoning problems. Choices B, C, D, and E are all valid implementation assumptions. Choice B questions whether enough people actually own cars or use them to drive to work. In the most basic sense, if people do not own cars the argument is irrelevant. Choice C highlights a lack of required opportunity to make a plan work. Public transportation must be both available and accessible should someone decide to switch. Choices D and E highlight unanticipated bottlenecks, namely, whether the current public transportation system can accommodate all the people who decide to switch, as well as meet financial requirements.

Problem 28   Rainbow Corporation

Choice B. If Tina is not aware of the recent newspaper articles featuring Rainbow Corp. as an environmental culprit, it does not make sense to conclude that she does not care about the environment. Choices A and C are irrelevant. In choice D, even if the company's public relations department didn't issue a statement denying that it violated the law, this does not mean that the company is guilty of any wrongdoing. Rainbow Corp.'s actual guilt or innocence has no impact on the issue at hand because Tina has no idea of the indictment. In choice E, the fact that Tina was a member of an environmental protection organization during her freshman and sophomore years in college weakens the claim a little, but not substantially.

Note: Let's review another example. Suppose that a certain global think tank is reviewing national anthems and the significance of their historical themes. It concludes that most national anthems have militaristic themes due in part to their creation during times of war or internal conflict. Therefore, the think tank recommends that in the context of preserving global peace and stability, countries should consider changing their national anthems to rid them of any militaristic references. What would weaken this claim? Any suggestion that citizens today are unaware of the presence of any militaristic themes in their countries' national anthems.

Problem 29 Personality

Choice C. A fundamental assumption is that business school interviewers can accurately identify the traits which lead to success in business school. If, for example, affability (friendliness) is a desired trait, then how will an interviewer judge whether a candidate possesses this quality? If intelligence is a desired trait, does this translate to looking for polished speaking ability, a perceived analytical mindset, or the ability to tell interesting stories? In general, how will an interviewer ascertain whether the candidate has a winning personality?

Choice A is a distortion. The interview may be an integral part of the interview process but not result, in and by itself, in a successful admissions effort. Good interviewing may be correlated with a successful admissions effort but not be the cause of a good admissions effort (i.e., correlation vs. causation). Also review Necessary vs. Sufficient Conditions, covered in *Chapter 5*. Good interviewing is likely a necessary but not a sufficient condition for a generally good admissions process.

Choice D is also a distortion. The interview need not have only one purpose. In addition to assessing candidates' personalities, interviewers might wish to seek clarification with respect to the applicants' backgrounds. Business schools might even use the interview as a public relations tool, helping to promote their schools so that in the event a candidate is accepted, the candidate would be more likely to accept the school's offer. In choice B, we don't know for sure whether the interview is the most important element in the admissions process.

With reference to choice E, there is no need for interviews to be held at similar times and places in order for them to be effective. Different interview venues do not necessarily imply inconsistency with respect to interview procedures or outcomes.

PROBLEM 30 YUPPIE CAFÉ

Proposed Solution in Outline Form

The argument concludes that you can use the Internet to advertise and make your business more profitable. The author uses as evidence the fact that Yuppie Café advertised on the Internet and its business increased by 15% over last year's total. I do not find this argument to be well reasoned, as it rests on several debatable assumptions.

Attacking the assumptions

- First, the argument assumes that a 15% increase in business is the same as a 15% increase in revenue or profit. The term "business increase" must be clarified in order to enable a proper comparison.
- Second, the argument assumes a cause-and-effect relationship between advertising on the Internet and the increase in business.

- Third, the argument assumes that Yuppie Café is representative of all other businesses—e.g., your own business.
- Fourth, the argument assumes that a company has the money to spend on Internet advertising and that the costs of Internet advertising do not outweigh the revenues to be received.

Attacking the evidence

- Will a 15% increase be achievable for an older, more mature business or just for a younger business, which is more likely to have significant year-to-year growth?

Conclusion

- In conclusion, to strengthen this argument, we need more information to substantiate the cause-and-effect, representative sample, comparison and analogy assumptions, and implementation assumptions mentioned above.
- We could also strengthen the argument by softening the absolute wording as used in the original argument. The original sentence states, "Their success shows you how you too can use the Internet to make your business more profitable." The wording could instead read, "Their success shows how you too can probably use the Internet to make your business more profitable," or "Their success shows how a number of companies can use the Internet to make their businesses more profitable."
- Finally, we need clarification as to what exactly the word "success" means. How is it defined?

Proposed Solution in Essay Form

The argument concludes that you can use the Internet to advertise and to make your business more profitable. The author uses as evidence the fact that Yuppie Café advertised on the Internet and its business increased by 15% over last year's total. I do not find this argument to be well reasoned, as it rests on several debatable assumptions.

First, the argument assumes that there is a cause-and-effect relationship between advertising on the Internet and an increase in business. It could be that Yuppie Café saw an increase in business for reasons not related to advertising on the Internet. For example, a major competitor of Yuppie Café may have gone out of business, the company may have started serving a higher-quality coffee product, business may have increased because word-of-mouth advertising lured customers, or perhaps there was a period of general economic prosperity.

Second, the argument assumes that Yuppie Café is representative of all other businesses, e.g., your own business. This creates a representative sample assumption. It may even be true that the Internet does help highly customer-oriented companies with their businesses, e.g., coffee shops, health spas, and book distribution companies. But what about an oil-and-gas or mining company? Obviously, it is difficult to generalize from a single example to all other companies.

Third, the argument assumes that other companies actually own computers, have access to the Internet in order to place company advertisements, and employ personnel capable of administering the system. Furthermore, the argument assumes that a company has the money or other financial wherewithal to spend on Internet advertising. Moreover, the argument assumes that the money a company spends on Internet advertising does not outweigh the revenues to be derived from increased sales. These considerations create implementation assumptions.

Fourth, the argument assumes that a 15% increase in business is the same as a 15% increase in profit. The word "business increase" likely refers to revenues, but, as we know, revenues and profit are not the same thing. Profit depends on the relationship between costs, revenues, and sales volume. Furthermore, the words "business increase" are vague. For example, a 15% increase in the number of customers served may not translate to a 15% increase in revenues or profits, particularly if the retail price of a cup of coffee has been significantly reduced or increased.

In conclusion, to strengthen this argument we need more information to substantiate the cause-and-effect relationship between advertising and an increase in business. We need more examples in order to show that Yuppie Café is not merely an exceptional business example. We need some assurance that companies have access to the Internet in the first place. We also need clarification as to whether an increase in business translates to an increase in revenues and/or whether an increase in revenues translates to an increase in profit.

One word—"success"—is particularly vague and needs clarification. Is a 15% increase in business a worthy criterion for "success"? To a venture capitalist, success might be defined by a return of 50% or more. Furthermore, should success be measured merely along a quantitative dimension? What about the qualitative dimensions of employee or consumer satisfaction? Finally, softening the wording in the original argument could strengthen the argument. The original sentence states, "Their success shows you how you too can use the Internet to make your business more profitable." The wording could read, "Their success shows how you too can probably use the Internet to make your business more profitable," or "Their success shows how a number of companies can use the Internet to make their businesses more profitable."

Chapter 5: Mastering Logic

PROBLEM 31   CHEMIST
Choice B. This problem highlights the fallacy of affirming the consequent. The circle representing chemists appears inside the bigger circle representing scientists, so all chemists are definitely scientists. But the reverse is not true. Not all scientists are chemists; other than chemists, there are many types of scientists, including biologists and physicists.

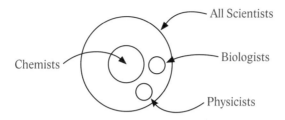

In choices A and D, the first part of each statement is correct while the latter half is incorrect. Choices C and E are both totally incorrect.

PROBLEM 32 INTRICATE PLOTS

Choice C. The last line of the introductory blurb gives us an "if...then" statement that serves as the passage's conclusion: "If scriptwriting is to remain a significant art form, its practitioners must continue to craft intricate plots." In determining what the author would most probably agree with, we need to look for logically deducible statements. Choice C, the correct answer, forms the contrapositive. "If a script does not have an intricate plot, it will probably not be a significant art form."

Choice A is an example of the fallacy of affirming the consequent, and tip #42 highlights this erroneous deduction. It is likely that other factors besides intricate plots also go into the making of a significant art form. Choice B is the fallacy of denying the antecedent. Choice D is outside the scope of the argument; we do not know whether scriptwriting is the most likely art form to become a significant one. Choice E is out. There is no reason to believe that more is better. Perhaps one intricate plot per script is enough.

PROBLEM 33 CAMPUS PUB

Choice D. This example highlights the fallacy of denying the antecedent. Looking back at the original, we find that just because it is not final exam week does not necessarily mean that the campus pub is not selling a lot of beer. For all we know, the campus pub sells a lot of beer every week because it is a popular pub. It is certainly likely that the campus pub does sell a lot of beer during final exam week, when students seek to relieve stress or celebrate. There could also be other lucrative weeks, particularly when sports matches such as football and basketball are being played.

In choice D, just because no one is happy doesn't necessarily mean some people won't smile. There could always be those people who smile regardless of whether they are happy or sad. Look at the original statement and concentrate on finding a similar structure.

Original Argument (fallacious):

final exam week → sell lots beer
(if it's final exam week, then the pub sells a lot of beer)

≠ final exam week → ≠ sell lots beer
(if it's not final exam week, then the pub does not sell lots of beer)

Now match this structure with correct choice D:

If happy → smile

≠ happy → ≠ smile

PROBLEM 34   BALCONY

Choice C. We are told that all apartments above the fifth floor have balconies. We cannot, however, logically infer that apartments on or below the fifth floor do not have balconies. Answer choices B and E provide tempting traps. For all we know, every apartment from the first floor on up has a balcony.

Tip #45 states that one way to think about an "If . . . then" statement in the form of "If A, then B" is that just because A leads to B does not mean that C, D, or E could not also lead to B. Case in point: The fact that increased expenditures on advertising have led to an increase in company sales does not mean that an increase in company sales could not have been achieved through other means—hiring more salespersons, lowering the retail price of products, or hiring a famous, talented manager.

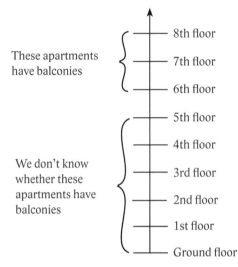

These apartments have balconies { 8th floor / 7th floor / 6th floor

5th floor

We don't know whether these apartments have balconies { 4th floor / 3rd floor / 2nd floor / 1st floor / Ground floor

Note: The statement, "If a person is rich, then he or she will vote in favor of a tax cut," does not mean that if a person is poor he or she will not also vote in favor of a tax cut.

PROBLEM 35   GLOBAL WARMING

Choice D. If we want to stop global warming then we must pass legislation. As highlighted in tip #46, we must draw an important distinction between necessary and sufficient conditions. Passing legislation is necessary to stop global warming, but it is not a sufficient condition for doing so. It is not a sufficient condition because several other factors probably are necessary to stop global warming. For starters, in all cases we may need more than just legislation; we may need legal enforcement of approved laws. Furthermore, choice C is a near-identical restatement of the original statement. Answer choices A and B are all correct interpretations of Jacques' original "If . . . then" statement. However, since Pierre believes Jacques' statement is not true, we must look for an erroneous answer choice.

Choice E is an opposite answer choice. Pierre's mistake consists in believing that legislation is the sole causal agent in stopping global warming (as opposed to one of several factors); his misunderstanding does not lie in the belief that legislation is an ineffective step toward stopping global warming.

Here's a related but simpler example:

JACQUES: If you want to keep your pet dog alive, you must give it water every day.

PIERRE: That's not true. It takes a lot more than water to keep your pet dog alive.

Pierre's response is inaccurate because he mistakenly believes that what Jacques has said is that

A) Giving water is necessary to keep your pet dog alive.
B) Only the giving of water will keep your pet dog alive.
C) If your pet dog is to be kept alive, it must be given water.
D) Giving water is enough to keep your pet dog alive.
E) Your pet dog will not be kept alive by giving it water.

Choice D above is, of course, the correct answer. Jacques's statement correctly identifies water as a necessary condition for keeping your pet dog alive. Pierre has mistakenly assumed that Jacques has said that water is a sufficient condition for keeping your pet dog alive.

PROBLEM 36   SALES

Choice C. Let's repeat what Debra said:

To be a good salesperson, one must be friendly.

Debra's statement above is also equivalent to the following:

If a person is a good salesperson, then he or she must be friendly.

Now let's summarize what Tom thought Debra said:

> If a person is friendly, then he or she will make a good salesperson.

Tom has effectively reversed the original "If . . . then" statement and erroneously committed the fallacy of affirming the consequent. Tom would have been correct had he instead responded, "Oh, what you mean is that only friendly people are capable of making good salespersons," or "I agree, a good salesperson must be friendly," or "That's right. If you're not friendly, then you're not going to make a good salesperson."

Choice B is a correct transcription of Debra's original statement. It cannot be correct because Tom disagrees with her. Choice E is a logical inference based on Debra's original statement (it is the contrapositive!). Choices A and D are not correct because regardless of whether the statements are true in themselves they do not lie at the crux of Tom's misunderstanding.

PROBLEM 37 FOOTBALL

Choice A. According to the rules of logical equivalency, the statement "Every person on the Brazilian World Cup football team is a great player," may be translated as, "If a person is on the Brazilian World Cup football team, then he is a great player." And this may be further translated as "Only great players are Brazilian World Cup football players." Although this latter statement sounds awkward to the ear, it is logically correct. "If A, then B statements" must be translated as "Only Bs are As" in order to be correct. See **Exhibit 5.5** on pages 144–145.

Choice A cannot be true. The statement "Only Brazilian World Cup football players are great players" is exactly what Beth has misunderstood Marie's remark to mean. Beth thinks Marie has said, "Brazil has all the great World Cup football players."

Choices B, C, D, and E are all unwarranted inferences.

PROBLEM 38   MEDICAL HIERARCHY

Choice A. With reference to the following diagram, the dotted circle representing researchers crosses into the solid inner circle representing surgeons, so we know for certain that at least some surgeons are researchers. Note that the solid circle representing surgeons is inside the larger solid circle representing doctors, which is inside the still larger solid circle representing medically licensed individuals.

For answer choices B through E, check for why each of these "could be true" and, in this way, eliminate them from contention as possible correct answers. Choice B could be true, as indicated by the area within the circle representing surgeons that appears above the dotted line (see embedded letter "B"). Choice C could be true, as indicated by the area outside the circle representing surgeons but within the circle representing doctors and within the dotted line (see embedded letter "C"). Choice D states basically the same thing as choice B. Some doctors/surgeons are researchers, but not all doctors/surgeons are researchers. Choice E could be true if the dotted circle extends beyond the solid circle representing medically licensed individuals (see embedded letter "E").

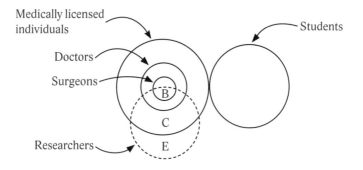

Problem 39   Valley High School

Choice E. With reference to the following diagram, if all physics students study math and no math students study French, then it must be true that no physics students study French. In referring to the diagram below, the little black circle (i.e., physics) must stay inside the larger black circle representing math students.

Again, the best way to eliminate wrong answer choices is to see which ones "could be true." Choice A is incorrect because the smaller dotted circle could be anywhere as long as it partially overlaps with the larger dotted circle representing English students. Choice B is incorrect because the little black circle representing physics students may or may not be within the larger dotted circle representing English students. Choice C is very tricky indeed because the small solid circle could be expanded to fit perfectly in the larger math circle. In this case, all physics students could be math students and all math students could be physics students, however unlikely. Choice D is also tricky. Should the large dotted circle representing English students be quite large, then it would be true that most math students study English but that most English students are not also studying math.

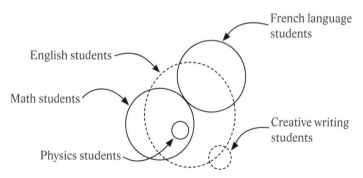

Appendix III: Avoiding Improper Inferences

Problem 40 Little Italy

1. Not inferable. We cannot infer that Antonio's restaurant is the best in the city. We could, however, infer that his restaurant is among the best Italian restaurants in the city. Note that the word "unsurpassed," both technically and legally, does not mean "best." It is possible that all products, competitors, etc., could be tied at number one and yet all could claim to be unsurpassed.

2. Not inferable. We can infer that Antonio is good at preparing Italian food, but we cannot infer logically that he "likes" preparing Italian food. He may in fact find preparing food very tedious and boring.

3. Not inferable. There is nothing to say that three out of every four Food and Beverage consultants do not also recommend a number of other Italian restaurants in the city. Which restaurant they recommend most is unclear.

4. Not inferable. This is a tad technical. "Antonio's customers prefer his style of Italian cooking by a ratio of 2 to 1." This original statement does not contain a logical comparative. In other words, it could be comparing Antonio's Italian cooking to mice, dog food, or to the common cold.

    The following is a statement from which a proper inference could be drawn: "Antonio's customers prefer his style of Italian cooking to that of other comparable Italian restaurants by a ratio of 2 to 1."

5. Not inferable. We simply do not know.

6. Not inferable. Tricky—even if Antonio is a connoisseur of Italian food, capable of preparing high-quality dishes, we do not know that he actually prepares high-quality food or whether he uses the highest-quality ingredients. For all we know, customers love Antonio's restaurant because of its location and ambience, not because the food is necessarily great. Note that the qualitative terms such as "well-known," "famous," or "successful" may not translate to their often-assumed monetary equivalents of "rich" or "profitable."

7. Not inferable. For all we know, Little Italy is a very popular restaurant even though it is inefficiently run and barely breaks even.

8. Not inferable. We cannot tell what would happen in another city or, for that matter, even in another location within Devon city.

9. Not inferable. We do not know. Customers may crowd the restaurant paying top dollar or they may fill the restaurant paying moderate prices.

10. Not inferable. Again, this is subtle. We may infer that Antonio spent a number of years preparing to become an Italian connoisseur, but he may have attained his reputation as an Italian connoisseur in a relatively short period of time.

Appendix IV: Analogies

PROBLEM 41 ANALOGY EXERCISE

1. RED is to PINK as BLACK is to GRAY. The relationship is one of intensity or degree. Pink is a muted form of red; gray is a muted form of black. Another way of saying this is that pink is red with a mixture of white and grey is black with a mixture of white.

   C. Type of Analogy: Degree

2. HEAT is to RADIATOR as BREEZE is to FAN. The relationship is that of the effect to its cause. Both wind and a fan can cause a breeze, so you must further refine the relationship. Artificial heat is produced by a radiator; an artificial breeze is produced by a fan.

   D. Type of Analogy: Cause and Effect

3. BIG is to LARGE as WIDE is to BROAD. High and long are dimensions, but they are not synonyms for WIDE. Small is an imperfect antonym. Broad means wide.

   B. Type of Analogy: Synonym

4. DOG is to CAT as CROCODILE is to LIZARD. Both a dog and a cat are part of a larger classification called "mammals." Both

a crocodile and a lizard are part of a larger classification called "reptiles." Both the hippopotamus and the elephant are mammals.

C. Type of Analogy: Part to Part

5. FLOWER is to BOUQUET as LINK is to CHAIN. A flower forms part of a bouquet as a link forms part of a chain.

D. Type of Analogy: Part to Whole

6. TOMORROW is to YESTERDAY as FUTURE is to PAST. This is a sequential relationship. By definition, the relationship of yesterday, today, and tomorrow is analogous to the past, present, and the future. Present occupies the wrong place in the sequence; it is analogous to today rather than yesterday. "Ago" is correct in its meaning but grammatically wrong.

B. Type of Analogy: Sequence

7. HERO is to VALOR as HERETIC is to DISSENT. The characteristic which makes one a hero is valor (courage); the characteristic which makes one a heretic is dissent from religious doctrine.

A. Type of Analogy: Characteristic

8. PRESENT is to BIRTHDAY as REWARD is to ACCOMPLISHMENT. A birthday is associated with receiving presents. An accomplishment is associated with receiving a reward. Medal and money are both types of rewards, not reasons for it.

A. Type of Analogy: Association

9. SKY is to GROUND as CEILING is to FLOOR. The roof is above the ceiling but is not opposite to it. Top and plaster are descriptive of ceiling.

A. Type of Analogy: Antonym

10. MONEY is to BANK as KNOWLEDGE is to BOOKS. One function of a bank is to hold money; one function of books is to hold knowledge.

   D.   Type of Analogy: Function or Purpose

Appendix V: The 10 Classic Trade-offs

PROBLEM 42   MATCHING EXERCISE

1.   **Fossil Fuels**
F.   **Short-term vs. Long-term trade-off**
Sometimes the only difference that stands between two opposing points of view is differing time frames. In other words, two people might well agree on a given solution but simply disagree as to when the solution might come about. In a short-term vs. long-term trade-off, two people agree on a given course of action but believe that it will be implemented during different time frames.

   In this example, two people argue that solar energy is the solution to our current energy needs: one person effectively says "I agree" and another says "I disagree." However, it is not that both persons disagree on solar energy's being a great alternative, but rather, they disagree on when it will become a viable alternative.

2.   **Miracle Tablets**
E.   **Quantity vs. Quality trade-off**
The issue here centers on how much pain reliever you get for your money. Quality equals the amount of pain reliever per tablet; quantity equals the price of a pain reliever, taking into consideration the number of tablets and their size.

   This problem is built on the assumption that you get twice the amount (quantity) of pain reliever for the same price, since Miracle tablets contain twice as much pain reliever with an identical price per bottle. Of course, the amount of pain reliever is a function of both the quality of pain reliever in each tablet as well as the number of tablets per bottle. The assumption, therefore, is that both competing bottles will contain the same number of tablets. If a bottle of regular aspirin contains twice as many tablets as a bottle of Miracle, the advantage effectively disappears.

What is likely the case here is that both bottles of pain reliever are the same size. Miracle tablets are twice as large as regular aspirin tablets, but a bottle of Miracle contains half as many tablets as a bottle of regular aspirin. In all likelihood, a Miracle tablet contains twice as much pain reliever per tablet compared with regular aspirin. Thus, it's all a wash. We're getting the exact same amount of pain reliever per bottle. Consumer's choice—would one prefer to take one big tablet or two small tablets to get the same amount of pain reliever?

3. Pirates
A. Breadth vs. Depth trade-off
According to this problem, music fans would be better served by a wider, costlier selection of music CDs than by a narrower, cheaper selection. This argument is grounded on the assumption that greater variety is better than less variety.

4. Techies
G. Specific vs. General trade-off
According to this argument, the reason people achieve top-level management jobs is that they develop analytically rigorous mindsets which come from their broader liberal arts–based education. All we have to do to weaken this argument is to suggest that vocationally trained individuals also develop analytically rigorous mindsets. For example, intensive training in a limited field such as computer programming may develop analytical skills as much as a broader liberal arts education does.

5. Workers
I. Theory vs. Practice trade-off
Working in an industry gives one practical experience. Studying an industry gives one a conceptual understanding of how that industry works. Working in an industry, however, does not guarantee that one understands the nuances of how that industry operates, especially at the macro level. Likewise, studying an industry does guarantee that one can grasp the nuances of how workers actually get things done in that industry. In this scenario, it is unclear whether those who work as union executives—college trained lawyers, economists, and labor relations officers—are incapable of grasping the inner workings of their industry (unionized labor). It is also unclear whether those who might come up through the ranks of the labor unions to become executives would be in a better position to manage and deal with the macro issues in which that industry operates.

6. Sales
D. Means vs. Ends trade-off
This problem pivots primarily on a "means vs. ends" trade-off and, in particular, on differing means. That is, the prospect of hiring more sales-people or conducting a market survey is based on differing means, while the decision to increase sales is based on an identical goal (end result).

7. Safe Haven
B. Control vs. Chance trade-off
The issue pivots on the difference between random violence and the violence that can be avoided by taking reasonable precautions. The conclusion that parents should not consider moving to the suburbs is weakened by the idea that parents exercise some control over their children's behavior while living in the suburbs. A parent has less of a chance to prevent teenage death due to a drive-by shooting than a death due to suicide or driving while intoxicated. This highlights a control vs. chance trade-off.

8. **Free Speech**
C. **Individual vs. Collective trade-off**

The argument basically says that free speech should know no limits. However, when free speech is deemed injurious to the collective rights of the "group," it is not allowed. In this respect, individual and collective rights trade-off with one another. We have free speech but in certain situations the rights of the group take precedence.

9. **Historians**
H. **Subjective vs. Objective trade-off**

Per the topic at hand, the historian's success in being scientifically objective is at best illusory because, here, objectivity is linked to detachment and is deemed incompatible with passion. Thus we have a subjective vs. objective trade-off.

10. **Discovery**
J. **Tradition vs. Change trade-off**

This problem gives rise to a rather interesting example, tying the tradition vs. change trade-off to argument by analogy. In this tradition vs. change trade-off, Nordwell was saying, "Okay let tradition prevail: I'll take Italy because Columbus took America." Likewise, according to argument by analogy, Nordwell was saying, "Because Columbus could claim America, I can claim Italy. But of course, I have no right to claim Italy, as Columbus had no right to claim America."

Appendix VI: Critical Reading and Comprehension

For an in-depth review of the strategies used to answer reading comprehension questions, including coverage of *The Four-Corner Question Cracker for Reading Comprehension*™, refer to *Appendix VII—Tips for Taking Reading Tests*.

PROBLEM 43   SAMPLE PASSAGE

Question 1
Choice D. This is an overview question. Look for the words of the topic and avoid overly detailed or overly general answer choices.

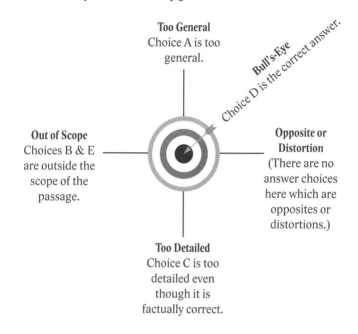

Too General
Choice A is too general.

Bull's-Eye
Choice D is the correct answer.

Out of Scope
Choices B & E are outside the scope of the passage.

Opposite or Distortion
(There are no answer choices here which are opposites or distortions.)

Too Detailed
Choice C is too detailed even though it is factually correct.

Choice A is too general because a discussion of educational philosophy in the last forty years would likely incorporate the viewpoints of many individuals, not just the author's viewpoint. Choice B is outside the passage's scope. We do not necessarily know whether or not teachers should receive more liberal arts training. Choice C is a correct statement within the passage's context. However, it is too detailed to satisfy the primary purpose as demanded by this overview question.

For an overview question, there are effectively five reasons why wrong answers could be wrong. An answer choice will either be outside a passage's scope, opposite in meaning, distorted in meaning, too general, or too detailed. Whereas choice C was too detailed, choice A is an overly general answer choice. It is very useful to be on the lookout for "out of the scope"-type answers. This was the fate of answer choices B and E. Note that opposites or distortions are not common wrong answer choices with regard to overview questions.

A time-honored tip for answering overview questions involves performing a "topic-scope-purpose" drill. That is, we seek to identify the passage's topic, scope, and purpose. Topic is defined as the passage's broad subject matter. It's an "article on education." The topic is therefore "education." Scope is defined as the specific aspect of the topic that the author is interested in. The scope here is "schooling versus education." Last, purpose is defined as the reason the author sat down to write the article. His purpose is to say: "Colleges or universities can't educate; they exist to prepare students for later learning because youth itself makes real education impossible."

Knowing the topic, scope, and purpose is enough to answer directly the question at hand. And knowing the author's purpose will likely set us up for another right answer on at least one of the remaining questions. Identifying the topic alone can help get us halfway to a right answer because the correct answer to an overview question almost always contains the words of the topic. In this case, the word "education" (or its derivative "educated") does not appear in answer choices B or E. We can feel fairly confident eliminating both of these choices.

Question 2
Choice E. This is an explicit-detail question which enables the reader to go back into the passage and effectively underline the correct answer. Look for a very literal answer.

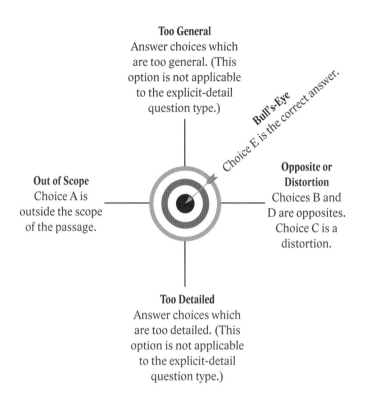

Too General
Answer choices which are too general. (This option is not applicable to the explicit-detail question type.)

Bull's-Eye
Choice E is the correct answer.

Out of Scope
Choice A is outside the scope of the passage.

Opposite or Distortion
Choices B and D are opposites. Choice C is a distortion.

Too Detailed
Answer choices which are too detailed. (This option is not applicable to the explicit-detail question type.)

Where is the correct answer to be found? Consider the words "prepare the young for continued learning in later life by giving them the skills of learning" (lines 10–11) and "better off if their schooling had given them the intellectual discipline and skill" (lines 21–22). The word "skill" surfaces both times that the author talks about what schools should be doing.

Choice A is outside the passage's scope. The passage does not talk about improving academic instruction or have anything to do with grassroots education levels. Nor does the passage talk about adults' opinions. Choice B is essentially opposite in meaning. To be correct, the answer choice should read, "redefine 'education' as 'schooling' so to better convey to parents the goals of teaching." The author feels that adults have missed the point in thinking that finishing school is the same as finishing one's education; in fact, schools exist to school, and education comes later. Choice D may be also classified as opposite in meaning, if we stick to the general spirit of the passage. The author believes that adults are very much uninformed and have missed the major point of education (lines 28–31); therefore closely implementing their opinions is essentially opposite to the author's intended meaning.

Choice C is a distorted meaning. Distortions are most often created by the use of extreme or categorical or absolute-type wordings. Here the word "only" signals a potential distortion. The author would likely agree that high scholastic achievement is a possible requirement for becoming educated, but not a sufficient condition in and of itself. In fact, the author really doesn't mention scholastic achievement, so we might classify it as being out of scope if we did not happen to focus initially on the absolute-type wording.

Question 3

Choice B. This is an inference question. The challenge is to find an answer that isn't explicitly mentioned in the passage, but can be logically inferred.

Although the author does not give an exact "education" formula, he effectively says that a number of factors are necessary to travel the high road to becoming educated. These include: passion, a knack for learning, discipline, and maturity. In terms of maturity, he clearly states, "The young can be prepared for education in the years to come, but only mature men and women can become educated, beginning the process in their forties and fifties and reaching some modicum of genuine insight, sound judgment and practical wisdom after they have turned sixty." Obviously, according to the author, if maturity begins in a person's forties and takes another ten to twenty years, then an individual cannot be less than forty years of age and still be considered educated.

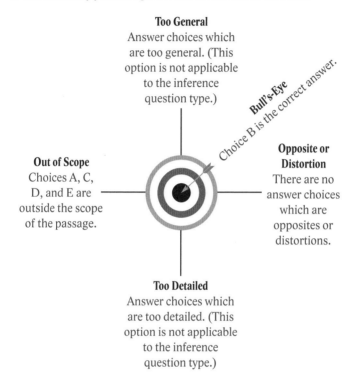

Too General
Answer choices which are too general. (This option is not applicable to the inference question type.)

Bull's-Eye
Choice B is the correct answer.

Out of Scope
Choices A, C, D, and E are outside the scope of the passage.

Opposite or Distortion
There are no answer choices which are opposites or distortions.

Too Detailed
Answer choices which are too detailed. (This option is not applicable to the inference question type.)

Wrong answer choices in inference-type questions often fall outside the passage's scope. Choice A is outside the passage's scope and is specifically referred to as an unwarranted comparison. The author does not say whether he believes becoming educated takes more passion than maturity or more maturity than passion.

Choice C is perhaps the trickiest wrong answer choice. The author doesn't imply that one has to be a university graduate. In fact, he mentions "school and/or college" (lines 3–4, 24, 26, and 28), which suggests that he may well lump high school in with college and/or university. A high school graduate might have enough schooling to get onto the road of education. Moreover, the author doesn't claim one must be a four-year college or university graduate or even whether one has to attend college or university.

There is no mention of classic works of literature, so choice D is outside the passage's scope; we cannot answer this question based on information presented in the passage. Choice E is wrong because the author never mentions "travel." Don't mistake the word "travail" (line 38, meaning "struggle") for "travel." Moreover, it is possible, without evidence to the contrary, that a person could never have left his or her own country and still understand those ideas that make him or her representative of his or her particular culture.

Question 4

Choice A. This is a tone question. Tone questions ask about the author's feeling or attitude toward someone or something in the passage. Basically, the author will be either positive, negative, or neutral. In most cases, especially with respect to social science passages (versus science passages), the fact that the author would sit down to write something hints that he or she has some opinion about the topic at hand. Therefore, the neutral answer choice is not usually correct, even if available.

For this question, we have, on the positive and supportive side, the word pairs "invaluable partners," "conscientious citizens," or "unfortunate victims." On the negative side, we have "uninformed participants" or "disdainful culprits."

The author's attitude toward adults is somewhat negative, but not excessively so. The feeling is more like frustration. The author believes that adults are ignorant of the distinction between schooling and education (lines 29–31). Therefore, positive-sounding choices C and D are out. Choice B, "unfortunate victims," is sympathetic, but the author thinks that adults are not victims, just misfocused. Choice E, "disdainful culprits," is too negative.

Question 5

Choice C. This is a passage organization question. Think in terms of the number of viewpoints and the relationships among them.

The author introduces his thesis or summary in the very first sentence—"a controlling insight in my educational philosophy"— then goes on to support it with his personal observations, experiences, and opinions. Thus, choice A is not correct. No objective analysis is put forth; if there were, we would expect to see some surveys, statistics, or alternative viewpoints introduced. Choice B is wrong because there is a single idea presented, but the author agrees with it because it is his own idea. Choice D is incorrect as there are not two viewpoints presented, just one. Choice E suggests a popular viewpoint, but it is highly unlikely that many people have adopted this viewpoint because, according to the author, adults (and, by extension, laypersons) haven't really caught on. Last, a number of perspectives are not drawn upon. The author chooses to spend the entire article developing his single viewpoint that "no one has ever been—no one could ever be—educated in school or college."

Quiz—Answers

1. **False.** Left-brain thinking might be described as "spotlight" thinking, while right-brain thinking might be described as "floodlight" thinking.

(See Divergent vs. Convergent Thinking; *Chapter 2: Creative Thinking*)

2. **False.** The formulaic relationship among the three elements of classic argument structure is:

   Conclusion = Evidence + Assumption

   or

   Conclusion − Evidence = Assumption

(See The ABCs of Argument Structure, *Chapter 4: Analyzing Arguments*)

3. **False.** The statement "some doctors are rich people" does imply reciprocality because "some rich people must be doctors."

(See Tip #50, *Chapter 5: Mastering Logic*)

4. **False.** The ad hominem fallacy consists in attacking the person, often in a personal or abusive way, rather than attacking the argument or claim being made. Attempting to draw attention away from the real issue describes the fallacy known as "red herring."

(See Ad Hominem vs. Red Herring, *Appendix II: Fallacious Reasoning*)

5. **False.** In formal logic, the phrase "Every A is a B" must be translated as "Only Bs are As," not "Only As are Bs." Case in point: The statement "Every cat is a mammal" must be translated as "Only mammals are cats." It is not true to say that if every cat is a mammal then only cats are mammals.

(See Tip #48, *Chapter 5: Mastering Logic*)

6. **False.** The halo effect is the tendency to view a person, place, or thing favorably based on only a single incident, trait, or characteristic.

(See The Magic of Coincidence, *Chapter 1: Mindset and Perception*)

7. **False.** The words "inference" and "assumption" are not the same and should not be used interchangeably. An "inference" is a logical deduction based on an argument, statement, or written passage. An assumption is an integral component of an argument.

(See *Appendix III: Avoiding Improper Inferences*)

8. **False.** Matrixes can be used to summarize data within a two-dimensional grid. Data must be "mutually exclusive and collectively exhaustive," not "collectively exclusive and mutually exhaustive."

(See Understanding Matrixes, *Chapter 3: Decision Making*)

9. **False.** Utility analysis takes into account the desirability of outcomes by multiplying each value by the probability of its occurrence. We do not total resultant values; we choose the outcome that yields the highest value.

(See Utility Analysis, *Chapter 3: Decision Making*)

10. **False.** The Prisoner's Dilemma provides an example of how cooperation is superior to competition.

(See Tip #19, *Chapter 3: Decision Making*)

Selected Bibliography

Adams, James L. *Conceptual Blockbusting: A Guide to Better Ideas*, 4th ed. Cambridge, MA: Perseus Publishing, 2001.

Adler, Mortimer and Geraldine Van Doren. *Reforming Education: The Opening of the American Mind*. New York: Macmillan, 1988.

Bennett, Deborah J. *Logic Made Easy: How to Know When Logic Deceives You*. New York: W.W. Norton, 2005.

Bransford, John D. & Barrry S. Stein. *The Ideal Problem Solver: A Guide for Improving Thinking, Learning, and Creativity*. 2nd ed. New York: Worth, 1993.

Buzan, Tony. *Use Both Sides of Your Brain: New Mind-Mapping Techniques*, 3rd ed. New York: Plume, 1991.

Cause, Donald C. & Gerald M. Weinberg. *Are Your Lights On? How to Figure Out What the Problem Really Is*. New York: Dorset House, 1990.

Copi, Irving M. & Carl Cohen. *Introduction to Logic*. 13th ed. Englewood Cliffs, NJ: Prentice Hall, 2008.

Damer, T. Edward. *Attacking Faulty Reasoning: A Practical Guide to Fallacy-Free Arguments*. Belmont, CA: Wadsworth, 2008.

de Bono, Edward. *The Use of Lateral Thinking*. New York: Penguin, 1986.

Harrison, Allen F. & Robert M. Bramson. *The Art of Thinking*. New York: Berkeley Books, 2002.

How to Prepare for the Graduate Record Examination: GRE General Test. 17th ed. Hauppauge, NY: Barron's Educational Series, 2007.

Jones, Morgan D. *The Thinker's Toolkit: 14 Powerful Techniques for Problem Solving*. New York: Times Books, 1998.

The Official Guide for GMAT Verbal Review. 2nd ed. Hoboken, NJ: Wiley, 2009.

Russo, J. Edward & Paul J.H. Schoemaker. *Decision Traps: The Ten Barriers to Brilliant Decision-Making and How to Overcome Them.* New York: Fireside, 1990.

Salny, Dr. Abbie F. & Lewis Burke Frumkes. *Mensa Think-Smart Book: Games and Puzzles to Develop a Sharper, Quicker Mind.* New York: Harper and Row, 1986.

Sternberg, Robert J. *Intelligence Applied: Understanding and Increasing Your Intellectual Skills.* Orlando, FL: Harcourt Brace Jovanovich, 1986.

Steinberg, Eve P. *Scoring High on Analogy Tests.* New York: Arco, 1990.

Stewart, Mark A. *GRE-LSAT Logic Workbook.* 3rd ed. New York: Arco, 1999.

Thomson, Anne. *Critical Reasoning: A Practical Introduction.* New York: Routledge, 2008.

Thouless, Robert H. *Straight and Crooked* Thinking. London: Hodder, 1990.

Weston, Anthony. *A Rulebook for Arguments.* 4th ed. Indianapolis, IN: Hackett, 2008.

Whimbey, Anthony & Jack Lockheed. *Problem Solving & Comprehension.* 6th ed. Hillsdale, NJ: Lawrence Erlbaum, 1999.

Wikipedia, *The Free Encyclopedia*, s.v. "Fallacy," http://en.wikipedia.org/wiki/Fallacy

Index

Numbers in *italics* (within parentheses) refer to problems and
exercises. They are preceded by corresponding page numbers.

ad hominem fallacy, 8, 161–2
Adler, Mortimer J., 182, 256
affirming the consequent, fallacy of,
    139–40, 168
analogies
    exercises, 173–75 (*41*)
    types of
        antonym, 171–72
        association, 173
        cause and effect, 172
        characteristic, 173
        degree, 172
        function or purpose, 173
        part to part, 172
        part to whole, 172
        sequence, 173
        synonym, 171
analytical thinking
    versus creative thinking, 25
appeal to pity fallacy of, 164
appeal to public opinion, fallacy of,
    164
arguments
    abc's of argument structure, 102–3
    defined, 101
    evaluating 103–8
    problems, 120–34 (*12–30*)
assigning irrelevant goals or
    functions, fallacy of, 163
assumptions
    defined, 101
    guide words, using, 102–3

problems
    cause and effect, 126–30
        (*19–24*)
    comparison and analogy,
        120–21 (*12–13*)
    "good evidence," 124–25
        (*17–18*)
    implementation, 130–33
        (*25–29*)
    representativeness, 122–24
        (*14–16*)
    types, overview of, 109–20

brainstorming
    business brainstorming
        questionnaire, 47–49
    generating ideas, 46
Buzan, Tony, 35, 256

cause and effect (causal
    oversimplification), fallacy of,
    167
circular reasoning, fallacy of, 161
coincidence
    "halo effect," link to, 8, 16
    Kennedy vs. Lincoln, case for,
        14–15
    Prince Charles and the Pope, 16
composition, fallacy of, 165
continuum, fallacy of the, 165
convergent thinking. *See* divergent
    thinking

creative thinking (creativity)
    inhibitors, 40–45
    lateral thinking, contrasted with, 25–29
    problems, 29–30 (*1–5*)
    selling creative ideas, 52
critical reasoning (thinking). *See* reasoning

de Bono, Dr. Edward, 25, 256
decision-event trees
    overview of, 72–75
    problem, 77 (*10*)
decision making
    "boxes" and "trees," 7, 55
    overview of, 55–56
denying the antecedent, fallacy of, 139–40, 169
devil's advocate technique, 37, 40
distinction without a difference, fallacy of, 160
distortion, fallacy of, 166
divergent thinking
    right-brain thinking and left-brain thinking, link to, 32–35
    versus convergent thinking, differences between, 31–32
division, fallacy of, 165
domino fallacy, 167

effective information paradigm, 68–69
equivocation, fallacy of, 160
evidence
    assumptions, linked to, 113–14
    defined, 101
    problems, 124–25 (*17–18*)

fallacies
    ad hominem, 161–62
    affirming the consequent, 139–40, 168
    appeal to pity, 164
    appeal to public opinion, 164
    assigning irrelevant goals or functions, 163
    cause and effect (causal oversimplification), 167
    circular reasoning, 161
    composition, 165
    continuum, 165
    denying the antecedent, 139–40, 169
    distinction without a difference, 160 distortion, 166
    division, 165
    domino fallacy, 167
    equivocation, 160
    false alternatives, 164
    false precision, 168
    faulty analogy, 167
    gambler's fallacy, 168
    golden mean, 164–65
    hasty generalization, 161
    incorrect attack on a generalization, 166
    negative proof, 161
    poisoning the well, 162
    red herring, 162
    tradition, 163
    tu quoque, 162
    wishful thinking, 163
false precision, fallacy of, 168
false alternatives, fallacy of, 164
faulty analogy, fallacy of, 167

gambler's fallacy, 168
golden mean, fallacy of the, 164–65

hasty generalization, fallacy of, 161

hypothesis testing
    overview of, 88–95
    type I and type II errors, 43, 92–95

ideas
    idea "growers," 45
    idea "killers," 44
    inhibitors to creativity, 40–42
incorrect attack on a generalization,
        fallacy of, 166
inferences
    avoiding improper, 169–70
    problem, 170–71 (40)

Kennedy, John F., 14–15

lateral thinking
    creative thinking vs. lateral
        thinking, 25–28
    de Bono, Dr. Edward, 25
    merchant and the money-lender,
        example of, 26–28
left-brain thinking vs. right-hand
        thinking, differences between,
        32–35
Lincoln, Abraham, 14–15
logic
    "if . . . then" statements, 138–41
        affirming the consequent,
            fallacy of, 139–40, 168
        denying the antecedent, fallacy
            of, 139–40, 169
    logical equivalency statement,
        144–45
    mutual inclusivity and exclusivity,
        142–43
    no-some-most-all statements, 8,
        141–42
    problems, 146–51 (31–39)
logical reasoning. See reasoning
lots-little matrix, 65–66

matrixes
    matrixes vs. tables, 66–69
    overview of, 9, 62–66
    problems, 71–72 (7–9)
mind maps
    Buzan, Tony, 35
    rules for creating, 36
    sample mind maps, 37–38
mindset
    four classic mindsets, the, 18–20
        analyst, defined, 19
        idealist, defined, 19
        realist, defined, 19
        synthesist, defined, 19
Muenzinger, K.F., 13

"out-of-the-box" thinking, 7, 26
    See also creative thinking

negative proof, fallacy of, 161

poisoning the well, fallacy of, 162
prisoner's dilemma, 9, 95–98
probability trees, 76–77
problem solving
    reframing problems, 50–51
    using creativity, 25
pros-and-cons analysis
    problem, 60 (6)
    using T-accounts, 56–61
public opinion, fallacy of, 164

reading comprehension
    reading skills, strategic review of
        common wrong answer choices,
            195–200
        passage content, 189–90
        passage question types,
            194–95
        passage structure, 190–93
        passage type, 188–89

reading tests, tips for taking,
185–87
sample passage, 182–85 (*43*)
reasoning
benefits of, 6–7
tips, summary of all, 155–59
reasoning flaws
five common, the, 109–20
red herring fallacy of, 162
right-hand thinking. *See* left-brain
thinking vs. right-brain thinking

selective perception
defined, 163
Socrates, 6
Sperry, Dr. Roger, 32
stereotypes
occupational work types, 21–22
selective perception, relating to, 13
sunk costs, 86–88

tips, summary of all, 155–56
trade-offs
exercise, identifying classic trade-
offs, 179–82 (*42*)

ten classic types, the
breadth vs. depth, 176
control vs. chance, 176
individual vs. collective, 176
means vs. ends,176–77
quantity vs. quality, 177
short-term vs. long-term, 177
specific vs. general, 177–78
subjective vs. objective, 178
theory vs. practice, 178
tradition vs. change, 178–79
tradition, fallacy of, 163
tu quoque fallacy, 162
type I and type II errors.
See hypothesis testing

utility analysis
understanding, 84–86

weighted ranking
formula for calculating, 78
problem, 83–84 (*11*)
understanding, 77–84
wishful thinking, fallacy of, 163

About the Author

Brandon Royal is an award-winning writer whose educational authorship includes *The Little Blue Thinking Book*, *The Little Red Writing Book*, *The Little Gold Grammar Book*, *The Little Red Writing Book Deluxe Edition*, *The Little Green Math Book*, and *Reasoning with Numbers*. During his tenure working in Hong Kong for US-based Kaplan Educational Centers—a Washington Post subsidiary and the largest test-preparation organization in the world—Brandon honed his theories of teaching and education and developed a set of key learning "principles" to help define the basics of writing, grammar, math, and reasoning.

A Canadian by birth and graduate of the University of Chicago's Booth School of Business, his interest in writing began after completing writing courses at Harvard University. Since then he has authored a dozen books and reviews of his books have appeared in *Time Asia* magazine, *Publishers Weekly*, *Library Journal of America*, *Midwest Book Review*, *The Asian Review of Books*, *Choice Reviews Online*, *Asia Times Online*, and About.com. Brandon is a five-time winner of the International Book Awards, a five-time gold medalist at the President's Book Awards, as well as a winner of the Global eBook Awards, the USA Book News "Best Book Awards," and recipient of the "Educational Book of the Year" award as presented by the Book Publishers Association of Alberta.

To contact the author:
E-mail: contact@brandonroyal.com
Web site: www.brandonroyal.com

Books by Brandon Royal

The Little Blue Thinking Book:
    50 Powerful Principles for Clear and Effective Thinking

The Little Red Writing Book:
    20 Powerful Principles for Clear and Effective Writing

The Little Gold Grammar Book:
    Mastering the Rules That Unlock the Power of Writing

The Little Red Writing Book Deluxe Edition

The Little Green Math Book:
    30 Powerful Principles for Building Math and Numeracy Skills

Reasoning with Numbers:
    Mastering the Thinking Skills That Unlock the Secrets of Basic Math

Secrets to Getting into Business School

Game Plan for the GMAT

Game Plan for GMAT Math

Game Plan for GMAT Verbal

Bars of Steel:
    Dancing for Your Life: The True Story of Maria de la Torre and Her Secret Life in a Hong Kong Go-Go Bar

Paradise Island:
    An Armchair Philosopher's Guide to Human Nature (or "Life Lessons You Learn While Surviving Paradise")

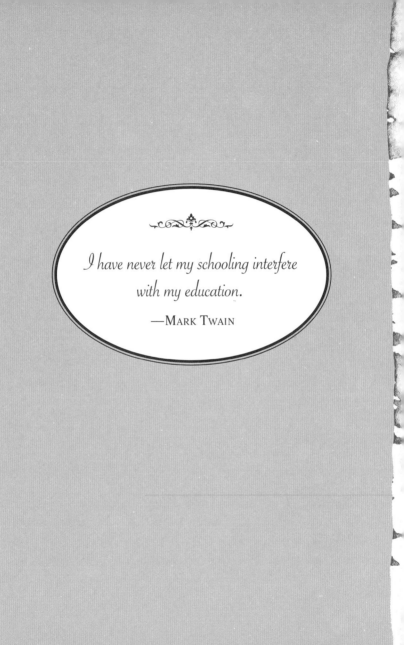

I have never let my schooling interfere with my education.

—MARK TWAIN